A History
of Professional
Writing Instruction
in American Colleges

SMU Studies in
Composition and Rhetoric
General Editor: Gary Tate,
Texas Christian University

A History of Professional Writing Instruction in American Colleges

Years of Acceptance, Growth, and Doubt

Katherine H. Adams

Southern Methodist University Press
Dallas

First edition, 1993

Requests for permission to reproduce material from
this work should be sent to:
  Permissions
  Southern Methodist University Press
  Box 415
  Dallas, Texas 75275
Some of the material in chapters 1 and 3 appeared in "Advanced
Composition: Where Did It Come From? Where Is It Going?" by
Katherine H. Adams and John L. Adams, an introductory essay to
Teaching Advanced Composition: Why and How, ed. Katherine H. Adams
and John L. Adams (Heinemann: Portsmouth, N.H., 1991), 3–15. Some
of the material in chapters 3 and 4 appeared in "The Paradox Within:
Origins of the Current/Traditional Paradigm," by Katherine H. Adams
and John L. Adams, *Rhetoric Society Quarterly* 17 (1987): 421–31.
Students' papers, teachers' notebooks, and class materials from Harvard
University are quoted by permission of the Harvard University Archives.

Library of Congress Cataloging-in-Publication Data
Adams, Katherine H., 1954–
    A history of professional writing instruction in American colleges
    : years of acceptance, growth, and doubt / Katherine H. Adams.—
    1st ed.
        p.   cm. — (SMU studies in composition and rhetoric)
    Includes bibliographical references and index.
    ISBN 0-87074-342-2
    1. English language—Rhetoric—Study and teaching—United States-
    -History.   2. Technical writing—Study and teaching—United States-
    -History.   3. Business writing—Study and teaching—United States-
    -History.   4. Creative writing—Study and teaching—United States-
    -History.   5. Journalism—Study and teaching—United States-
    -History.   I. Title.   II. Series.
    PE1405.U6A33   1993
        808'.042'071173—dc20   92-35966

For my sister
Laura

Contents

Preface   *ix*

1   Advanced Writing Instruction and the Shift from College to University   *1*

2   "The Cry for More English"   *16*

3   At Harvard and Beyond: Advanced Composition as a Composite Course   *36*

4   The First Specialized Courses and Course Arrays   *61*

5   Teaching Creative Writing   *70*

6   Education for Journalism   *99*

7   "Professional Writing" in Agriculture, Engineering, and Business   *123*

8   Conclusion   *147*

Works Cited   *155*

Index   *171*

Preface

Today college graduates work as writers at newspapers, magazines, advertising offices, television studios, college alumni offices, banks, power plants, hospitals, and everywhere else. Some of them have no training in writing beyond freshman composition, but most have taken at least one or two advanced courses in journalism, technical writing, ad copy writing, public relations writing, business writing, creative writing, advanced composition, or writing across the curriculum.

Although advanced writing courses are now separated into different divisions and departments, they were begun between 1880 and 1910 by a small group of English teachers, many of whom worked with more than one course. These classes have had similar—if separate—histories since then, similar periods of growth, similar successes and problems arising from the shared mission of training students to be writers. At different times, critics have argued about all these divisions that the courses are too concerned with the students' own psyches or too concerned with their careers; that they involve too much or too little reading; that they make up no clear sequence or too controlled a sequence; that they are too small a part of the college curriculum or too large. Besides these ongoing debates and the curricular alterations ensuing from them, professional writing faculties have shared uncertainties concerning their academic status and problems with student recruitment and placement.

This common history has been given little scholarly attention. Two books from the 1930s discuss the first college classes in journalism (O'Dell, Nash). Robert Connors's article in the *Journal of Technical Writing and Communication* surveys the history of technical writing instruction. Other studies explain how one type of writing developed at one school, such as journalism at the University of Missouri, creative writing at the

University of Iowa, and business writing at the University of Illinois (S. Williams, Wilbers, Weeks). But no study has looked at the development of the entire college curriculum in advanced or professional writing. Certainly few teachers in one division know much about any other.

This book will survey that history beginning with the nineteenth-century change from general to specialized college training, a revolution in education from which today's varieties of advanced writing instruction have evolved. It will next move to the first composite advanced composition courses and then to those that took on each genre separately, an array of classes developed between 1890 and 1910 by a few teachers at a few schools. Subsequent chapters will consider each of these types of training separately, surveying their development after they split from each other but also pointing to the similarities in their growth.

This history, of a massive effort to train writers, is worthy of study not only because of the individual teachers and students involved in it, but also because of its possible impact on our current writing curricula. In the early 1900s, English department advanced writing courses began to split from each other in recognition of the specialties of incoming writing teachers and the requirements of different writing jobs or interests, with the teachers and students involved with fiction, for example, becoming separated from those studying journalism or business writing. But professional writing has been moving away from such strict divisions, if they ever really existed, and into fusions like New Journalism, a more informal style of technical writing, prose poetry, nonfiction novels, and "fictional" styles of literary nonfiction. Journalists, magazine writers, business and technical writers, advertising and public relations specialists, and other types of writers need to know not only about the news article or letter form, but also about the possibilities created by personal examples, poetic imagery, characters, dialogue, interviews, stories, essay structures, emotional and logical appeals, and primary and secondary research—about techniques and skills now the property of several departments and programs.

Because these programs have generally remained separate and because they compete for the same students and the same academic authority, writing teachers across campus often seem leery of each other at best. But the difficult effort of teaching students to write has not been furthered by characterizations of muddleheaded creative writers or one-column-of-fragments journalism teachers or form-letter business and technical writing teachers or grammar-fixated composition teachers or snooty, troublemaking rhetoricians. We need to recognize our common beginnings and talk about our respective strengths with the goal of training today's students to be writers.

I would like to thank the colleagues who have helped me with this project. At Loyola University/New Orleans, I have tried out many of my half-formed notions on Ray Schroth of the communications department and John Biguenet of the English department. I am indebted to Mike Keene of the University of Tennessee for sharing his knowledge of technical writing and to Sue Simmons of Bowling Green State University and David Russell of Iowa State University for helping me with archival research. Two of my students at Loyola—John Davis and Elise Bordes—served as excellent bibliographic assistants. Avia Morgan, as always, made the manuscript production possible. I also want to thank Loyola University's fine reference librarians, Jim Hobbs, Mark Sutton, and Diana Madonna, who, along with Pat Doran, our very competent and patient interlibrary loan officer, provided me with invaluable service.

I would also like to thank Southern Methodist University Press and Loyola University's Committee on Grants and Leaves for the financial support that allowed me to travel to various university archives.

My greatest thanks goes to Gary Tate, a most incisive editor.

1

Advanced Writing Instruction and the Shift from College to University

In 1800 as in 1750, at the 25 or so colleges situated along America's east coast, students learned rhetorical principles and made oral presentations during four years of a fairly uniform liberal arts curriculum. Additional career training, usually for law or the church, came through apprenticeship. By 1900, at the more than 750 universities, colleges, and technical institutes across the country, students generally took liberal arts courses in their first two years and then chose among tracks in engineering, agriculture, education, library science, business, home economics, the humanities, and other fields for their course work of the last two years. This revolution in higher education triggered a revolution in the teaching of writing. As more students entered college, as specialties grew in number, and as students began to perceive college as a direct route toward various careers, the four years of required work in rhetoric that had been a key part of the earlier classical curriculum dwindled into two semesters of basic or remedial composition for freshmen. The history of advanced composition instruction, then, begins with higher education's abandonment of traditional rhetoric training—at a time when business, scientific, and news writing were becoming crucial to an expanding nation.

Professionalizing the College Education

At its beginnings in the mid-seventeenth century and throughout the eighteenth century, American higher education relied
on the medieval and Renaissance model of the *trivium* and
quadrivium: classical logic, grammar, and rhetoric, and the
lesser arts of arithmetic, geometry, astronomy, and music. Students also continued their religious training: except for the College of Pennsylvania in Philadelphia, all of the colonial colleges
were founded and supported by religious groups. During this
period, a common pattern was for each day or half-day to be
devoted to one subject, as in Harvard's 1652 curriculum,
which stipulated that philosophy be taught on Monday and
Tuesday, Greek on Wednesday, Hebrew on Thursday, rhetoric
on Friday, and catechism on Saturday (Rudolph, *Curriculum*
32), thus creating a time allotment like the following:

> Eighteen percent of the time was spent on Greek, 18 per-
> cent on Hebrew and other Eastern tongues, 18 percent on
> rhetoric, 9 percent on logic, and 9 percent on divinity. Now
> if these are together into what we would call Humanities,
> they amount to a total of 72 percent of the curriculum.
> In contrast, 15 percent was devoted to mathematics and
> science—12 percent to arithmetic, geometry, and astron-
> omy, and 3 percent to physics (largely Aristotelian); and
> .5 of 1 percent to botany which was offered on Saturday af-
> ternoons in the summers. What we might call the social
> sciences or the social studies included 12 percent of the
> student's time that was devoted to ethics and politics (Aris-
> totle) and .5 of 1 percent to history on Saturday afternoons
> in the winter. (Butts 28)

Much of the teaching was done by tutors, recent graduates
"very poor and very pious" (A. White 466), who three times a
day listened to recitations of textbooks and lecture notes.
Looking back on his undergraduate experience at Yale, Andrew
D. White, Cornell's first president, observed, "The minds of
the students were supposed to be developed in the same manner as are the livers of the geese at Strasburg—every day sundry
spoonfuls of the same mixture forced down all throats alike"

(465). This system of lecture and recitation allowed for a high student/teacher ratio. It also had the backing of the current educational theory derived from faculty psychology, which asserted that students needed to develop their memories thoroughly, through recitation, before improving their powers of judgment.

Before the Revolutionary War, the rhetorical precepts assigned for memorizing came from Peter Ramus. Using the *Rami Logica,* students studied argument types such as definition, comparison, and division. For their work on style, they memorized definitions and examples of the tropes and figures of speech listed in textbooks by his disciples, Omer Talon and William Dugard (Guthrie 49–50). To supplement this recitation and study of theory, teachers gave some attention to the individual student's ability to give speeches and write. For monthly and quarterly exercises, senior examinations, and other special academic occasions such as commencement, students performed orations in Latin, Greek, Hebrew, and sometimes English. They could also participate in disputations conducted at monthly meetings and on special occasions. Using syllogistic logic learned from Ramus and other sources, students might defend or attack a given statement of universal truth, considering, for example, "old brain-teasers" like

> whether animals think, whether the human mind is always thinking, whether all human actions are voluntary, whether the Scriptures are divinely inspired, whether a promise extorted by force is binding, whether everything that happens is for the best, whether there are any innate ideas, whether man can sin while sleeping. (Morgan 395)

By 1750, knowledge of the inductive scientific method, crucial to the new sciences being introduced into American colleges, as well as the desire for practice with realistic public discourse, spelled the end of syllogistic disputations in Latin. By 1782 Yale held inductive forensic disputations in English every Tuesday and three Mondays per month. For these exercises, teams of two or four debated current issues instead of abstract moral questions. In 1767, at King's College, as Columbia University was originally called, students considered whether a man ought to engage in war if he were not persuaded of the justice of the cause. In 1773, at Harvard, a key issue was the legal and moral ramifications of slavery. In 1779, Yale seniors centered their commencement debates on the justice of imposed taxations. For all these topics, students brought forth facts and examples to support their positions (Rudolph, *Curriculum* 45–47).

This emphasis on a more practical form of argumentation was reflected in the commonly used texts. After the Revolutionary War, Ramus's popularity waned quickly. Instead of learning his figures and tropes, students read George Campbell's *Philosophy of Rhetoric* (1776) to examine intellectual and emotional appeals and Hugh Blair's *Lectures on Rhetoric and Belles Lettres* (1783) to consider the role of rhetoric in literary criticism, poetry, historical writing, and other belles-lettres; Richard Whately's *Elements of Rhetoric* (1828) entered the curriculum later to guide the study of forensic argumentation (Kitzhaber 81–89; N. Johnson 19–63). The four years' work often contained a progression from grammatical skills to belles-lettres to argumentation. In 1820 at Harvard, for example, the texts included Walker's *Rhetorical Grammar* and Lowth's *English Grammar* in the freshman year, Cicero's *De Oratore* and the two volumes of Blair in the sophomore year, and Hedge's *Logick* in the junior year. In 1833 at Harvard, students studied Greek and Latin, mathematics, and history in the freshman year, read Lowth and Whately in the sophomore year, wrote themes and forensics in the junior year, and continued their writing in the senior year while attending lectures on rhetoric and criticism.

The texts and disputation types had changed by the beginning of the nineteenth century, but instruction still followed the colonial model: students attended weekly lectures on each subject that were conducted by the president and a few tutors, did recitations of textbook materials, and participated voluntarily in weekly or monthly oral disputations. By this time, the themes and forensics were usually written in English, with the assigned topics often drawn from other course work. Theme topics at Harvard in the 1850s, for example, included the following questions: Tarquin the Proud—is his place in history deserved or a gift from fortune? How would you compare the liberty of Athens and America? What appears to be the most exciting topic of the day? What are the merits and faults of the American newspaper? Forensic exercises were drawn from ongoing political and social debates: Does isolated America need army and navy fortifications? Should a congressman submit his own opinions to those of his constituents? Can a lawyer be justified in defending the guilty? Was the state legislatures' confiscation of Tory property justifiable? The teacher or assistant marking the papers, not necessarily the same one who lectured on text materials and heard recitations, would circle spelling errors but did not provide detailed critiques (Potter).

This early college curriculum in the humanities was pursued by a select few. Each class was small: in 1775 Harvard graduated 40; Yale, 35; Columbia, 13; Dartmouth, 11; and Pennsylvania, 8 (Wilson and Dobbins 241). In 1770, out of a population of 3,000,000, there were only 3,000 living alumni of American colleges (*Missions of the College Curriculum* 20). These men became leading doctors, ministers of the largest churches, statesmen, and judges.

For these few graduates, such an education did have its practical or vocational side. Lawyers, doctors, and clergymen needed to be able to read classical languages. Their professional status was also increased by knowledge of English belles-lettres, classical literature, and philosophy, and by their skill with written and spoken argumentation. But, of course, this college training was only partially or indirectly vocational, and it was not required for entering any profession. Prospective lawyers could attend college lectures on politics, civil government, and international law, but their practical career training occurred through apprenticeships, without the requirement of a college degree (Stevens 3–4). Similarly, to apprentice as a doctor or enter a private medical school, a young man did not have to have attended college. As late as 1900, an average of one year of high school was required for admission to an American medical school; only Johns Hopkins and Harvard had begun requiring college preparation (Parsons 473). In private academies and public high schools, students found education in classical and modern languages, history, composition, science, and mathematics as well as vocational training in surveying, navigation, bookkeeping, and agriculture (Popham 141). Only the most ambitious or wealthy went from there to college.

By the middle of the nineteenth century, the traditional curriculum leading to the liberal arts degree, valued because it "endowed those who completed it with cultural attributes that were signs of superior status," began to seem increasingly irrelevant in an industrializing nation no longer dominated by a few upper-class clerics and statesmen (Handlin and Handlin 10). New merchants and businessmen eschewed college training as effete, not relevant. Brown University's Francis Wayland concentrated on this problem in his 1850 report to the college corporation:

> Lands were to be surveyed, roads to be constructed, ships to be built and navigated, soils of every kind, and under every variety of climate, to be cultivated, manufactures were to be established. . . . What could Virgil and Horace and Homer and Demosthenes, with a little mathematics and natural philosophy, do towards developing the untold resources of this continent? (*Report to the Corporation* 12–13)

Also in 1850, the Massachusetts General Court urged Harvard to abandon its classical curriculum, to begin giving citizens the more practical, open curriculum they wanted, and to pay professors by class size: "Those only would succeed who taught . . . in a manner acceptable to the public. That which was desired would be purchased, and that which was not, would be neglected" (Rudolph, *Curriculum* 102). At that time Ralph Waldo Emerson often spoke at college literary clubs, usually at off-campus meetings, complaining of the college's neglect of individual talents and ambitions, of its dullness that left graduates disillusioned and unfit for careers (Bledstein 259–68).

The colleges gradually began to respond to such criticisms with various alterations influenced by the German university system: a wider array of subject fields, elective choices, programs in science and math, and more vocational courses. Cornell University opened in 1866 with classes in agriculture, mechanical arts, civil engineering, commerce and trade, mining, medicine and surgery, law, education, and public service. Yale and Harvard established separate scientific schools that offered training in chemistry, physics, metallurgy, and engineering. By 1900 the University of Michigan listed metallurgy, drawing, industry, and commerce among its liberal arts departments. At Harvard, president Charles Eliot began allowing students to choose among the newer and older offerings within Harvard College: "by 1872 the senior year at Harvard had become completely elective, then the junior year in 1879, and sophomore in 1884" (Eddy 60). Other schools also established an elective system that enabled students to combine liberal arts with new scientific and career-oriented courses.

In these experiments, a key ingredient was the training for vocations, for newer professions such as engineering and business that were crucial to national growth and that sought a status equal to that of the older professions of law, medicine, theology, and education. This change was met with opposition from traditional academics, guardians of the liberal arts curriculum who quickly acted to keep vocational programs and students separate from the older college. At Yale, students from the Sheffield Scientific School could not sit in chapel or in the dining hall with students of Yale College. Since this separate scientific college had lower entrance standards and a three-year, vocational course of study, its students were considered "second-class citizens, too benighted to aspire to the only worthy degree and therefore to be treated with condescension" (Rudolph, *American College and University* 232). The situation at Yale was a common one: "Actually, although these schools bore the university's name, they lived a life apart; supported by their fees, controlled by their own separate staffs, imposing their own lax requirements, physically out of sight, and altogether out of mind except at commencement time" (Capen 138). But however disparaged or isolated or underfunded, these professional programs continued to grow since they offered struggling universities the opportunity to serve important new constituencies and thus to gain needed political and economic support.

Paramount in this transfer to professional training were the land grant colleges, established under the provisions of the Morrill Act of 1862. This legislation granted to each state 30,000 acres of federal land for each congressman from the state. The land was to be sold to provide

> the endowment, support, and maintenance of at least one college where the leading object shall be, without excluding other scientific or classical studies, to teach such branches of learning as are related to agriculture and the mechanic arts, in such manner as the legislatures of the States and Territories may respectively prescribe, in order to promote the liberal and practical education of the industrial classes in the several pursuits and professions of life. (Ross 46–47)

By 1862, the grant had been given to five private colleges, including Sheffield at Yale and MIT, and eight state schools, and it had funded four new agricultural colleges. Forty-three land grant schools had been created by 1879 by assigning funds to existing private colleges and state universities and by establishing new institutions, including six separate colleges for blacks. By 1899, five more state universities, eight new agricultural and mechanical colleges, and 11 new black colleges joined this list (Eddy 49–50, 83). These schools generally offered curricula in engineering and agriculture for men and in home economics for women as well as traditional humanities courses, often to the dismay of professionals in industry and agriculture who had envisioned purely technical training.

With the numbers and sequences of professional courses increasing, an elective system did not seem adequate for insuring thorough career training. In recognition of these specialties, many colleges began to institute "majors" and other requirements. By 1901, Yale had begun moving to a system of concentration and distribution, a combination of a primary field of study and courses chosen from different disciplines. In 1905 Cornell abandoned its elective system and began requiring that 20 percent of the student's course work be taken in four specified fields (Rudolph, *Curriculum* 228–29). By 1920 most universities had instituted degree programs consisting of a major, a general education requirement, and electives (Veysey 10).

The University of North Carolina, one of the country's first state universities, provides an example of these changes in American higher education, from the classical curriculum of the colonial period to the addition of scientific and vocational courses in the late nineteenth century to the system of majors and electives in the twentieth. The first trustees in 1792 advocated a combination of a classical curriculum with practical laboratory instruction in the sciences and agriculture. The 1795 curriculum, however, mirrored that of most colleges: English grammar and Roman antiquities for the first year; arithmetic, geography, and Greek classics for the second; mathematics, natural philosophy, and astronomy for the third; and logic, moral philosophy, history, and belles-lettres for the fourth. Although the university's first enrollee, Hinton James, became a civil engineer, he did not receive his vocational training in college.

In 1850, the majority of a University of North Carolina student's time was still given to a set curriculum in Latin, Greek, mathematics, modern languages, rhetoric, and logic, but students could also attend regular lectures in chemistry, geology, botany, zoology, psychology, and political science. No laboratory work was required in the sciences, but professors of chemistry and physics did perform experiments for their classes. In 1854 the university opened its School for the Application of Science to the Arts to train engineers, chemists, farmers, and miners. Although the regular enrollees could take engineering or agricultural chemistry during the second semester of their senior year, the science school was mostly kept separate: it had different entrance requirements and offered a two and one-half year degree. Because of such practical programs, the university received the state's Morrill Act funding, using it, as many schools did, to pay general expenses during the difficult postwar period (Battle I 552–53, 642, 756–57).

But, even with that funding, the university could not stay open: it closed from 1871 to 1875 largely because its classical curriculum seemed useless, irrelevant, to most of the state's citizens. At its formal reopening in 1888, the university instituted separately administered schools—with salaries to be funded from their tuitions (Battle I 765–66). The new colleges—literature and the arts; philosophy, chemistry, and natural history; science and the arts; agriculture and the mechanical arts; business and commerce; normal college; law; and medicine—set their admissions standards and designed their curricula to meet the needs of their own constituencies. The professional programs flourished and soon a teacher's training course, graduate degrees in the arts and sciences, and a college of pharmacy were added. An agricultural experiment station opened in 1877 (Eddy 77). These programs at first existed within an elective system, which by 1895 applied to all studies of the senior year, half of the junior, and two-fifths of the sophomore (Battle II 509). In 1905, undergraduates could take traditional humanities and lab science courses as well as money and banking, transportation, labor, hydraulics, sanitary engineering, mechanical drawing, and electric wiring, often in combinations of their own devising (Rudy 19). But such freedom was short-lived: by 1910 schools and departments began insisting on regulated combinations of courses in liberal arts and in the student's major. Like many other schools, the University of North Carolina had come the long distance from a classical curriculum to a system of majors and electives, in which students pursued different degrees having different requirements.

The Impact on Writing

Students of the late nineteenth century preparing for various careers were not interested in and did not receive the four years' training in rhetoric given to earlier generations. With each succeeding decade, the colleges required fewer rhetoric courses and less additional theme and forensic writing. At Brown in 1870, juniors pursuing humanities degrees still did declamations, but seniors studied English and American history. At Hobart College in 1879, juniors in the liberal arts program studied the English language, Anglo-Saxon grammar, Chaucer, and Spenser and did orations; seniors studied debate and Shakespeare and Milton (Wozniak 72–74). By 1900 both schools had distribution requirements in the humanities that included literature and linguistics, but no required work in rhetoric. At the University of North Carolina, the earlier requirements in English grammar, classical rhetoric, belles-lettres, and logic were replaced by English literature and speech classes as elective choices by 1900.

As departments and majors formed, English professors, often trained in specialized graduate programs, turned their attention away from rhetoric to a growing number of courses in linguistics and English and American literature. At the University of Pennsylvania in 1850, for example, seniors heard lectures on English literature as their only study of nonclassical literature. In 1869–70, juniors in the bachelor of arts program studied the English language, and seniors surveyed English literary history. In 1880–81, sophomores read Samuel S. Haldeman's *Outlines of Etymology* and Thomas R. Lounsbury's *English Language,* juniors could study Shakespeare as an elective, and seniors could study Chaucer, Spenser, or Hippolyte Taine's *History of English Literature.* In 1890–91, sophomores were required to take two courses, Modern Essayists and Modern Novelists, juniors took English Literature from Dryden to Cowper, and seniors took The Elizabethan Period and Modern and Contemporary Poets. Courses concerning English prose authors, English philology, Old English, Middle English, and comparative linguistics could also be taken as electives. By 1900, no literature was required of seniors, but the department had added electives on English drama, English versification, Chaucer, Anglo-Saxon, and phonetics.

By the turn of the century, as literary and linguistic offerings increased, extended rhetorical training was no longer even an elective option. The written notes and oral performances necessitated by the older system of class recitation were also gone (Russell 39–40). But teachers and administrators did recognize the need to offer basic instruction in writing for students entering college with increasingly varied, and often insufficient, educational backgrounds. To help Harvard students reach the crucial "college level," A. S. Hill began to urge that required courses be instituted at the freshman and sophomore levels, providing drill in "the habitual use of correct and intelligent English" (Copeland and Rideout 2). By 1884, other Harvard administrators and teachers recognized that the elective system had led to insufficient writing instruction and practice and thus to inadequate skills, and they first responded by requiring composition classes and theme writing in all four years.

In 1884–85, students in the new freshman requirement, a course moved from the sophomore year and labeled English A, met three hours a week for lecture sessions on sentence forms, paragraphing and essay writing, English literature, and Hill's *Principles of Rhetoric*. This class introduced them to the forms of discourse—narration, description, and argument in the first edition of Hill's text, with a fuller treatment of these three and added materials on exposition provided in his 1895 revision. Course B, which was required for all sophomores and met for a half hour each week, entailed further instruction on exposition in the first half year and on description and narration in the second, with Barrett Wendell's *English Composition* as the text. Course C, prescribed for juniors, met for two hours a week until November 15 and then for one hour a week for the rest of the year. In this class, students heard lectures on argumentative composition and wrote briefs and formal arguments. Course D, prescribed for seniors, continued the students' work on argumentation (Harvard College, Catalogue 1884–85 85–86; Catalogue 1885–86 89; *Announcement of the Department of English* 4–6). In all three of the advanced classes, attendance was voluntary; the theme writing was required. By 1900, Harvard's English teachers had reconsidered this composition requirement, deciding that they had mandated too extended a commitment for students and too much labor for faculty. They then stipulated a single year's requirement, Course A, which contracted the work on grammar, paragraphing, and the four forms of discourse from the earlier four-course sequence.

When Barrett Wendell taught English A in 1889–90, as his teaching notebook indicates, his lectures were drawn from Hill's *Principles of Rhetoric* as well as Bain's *English Composition and Rhetoric,* Hodgson's *Errors in the Use of English,* Bigelow's *Handbook of Punctuation,* and Carpenter's *Exercises in Rhetoric and English Composition.* To begin the year, he spent a day each on good use, barbarisms, improprieties, kinds of words, types of sentences, and solecisms. He then taught unity, mass, and internal structure, principles he applied to sentences, paragraphs, and essays. In the margin of his note-book, he commented on his creation of terms that, with "internal structure" relabeled as "coherence," became a mainstay of freshman texts and courses:

> Now the principles of composition have grouped them-selves in my mind under three heads:
> A. That which concerns the substance of a composi-tion—unity
> B. concerns outline—mass
> C. internal structure—unity of sentence, paragraph, whole composition.
> These not very satisfactory names are my own. I do not de-fend them, save on the grounds that any name is better than none, & that these are the names that some years of practice as a critic of undergraduate style have got me into the habit of using in every-day work.

In January, his lectures focused on clearness, force, and ele-gance of style. Then, from February until the end of the spring term, he turned his attention to the four forms of discourse. Throughout the year, he also assigned literary readings and analysis papers (Notes for English A).

Most schools never instituted the upper-level composition re-quirements found at Harvard in the 1890s, but they did create a freshman sequence in which students studied grammar, para-graphing, rhetorical modes, and writing about literature. By the early 1900s, students in their first semester at Harvard and many other schools wrote autobiographical themes, did a li-brary exercise, defined a term, described how to make or do something, wrote an exposition, defended or attacked a current opinion, and did a contrast or analogy paper. During the second term, they wrote reports and analyses concerning literature, fre-quently on Shakespeare, Thackeray, and Eliot (Wozniak 131). By 1910, Princeton was the only major eastern school that had not instituted such a requirement. In creating a two-semester sequence, universities were attempting to dispense with com-position problems quickly so that students could proceed to their majors and electives. Beyond this basic training, a few English departments maintained electives in rhetoric or a theme-writing requirement, along with an increasing number of courses concerning literature and linguistics.

Little Writing Instruction—But Professional Writers Needed

In this time of vocational education, and of very little rhetorical training, the profession of "writer" was becoming established in America—especially at the newspaper and magazine. In fact, the number of dailies increased from 1,489 in 1870 to 2,250 in 1914, a time when newspaper production involved more reporters than ever before. Circulation totals for all daily publications rose from 2.6 million copies in 1870 to 15 million in 1900, as the proportion of subscribers went from 10 percent to 26 percent of the adult population. By the mid-nineties, the largest American paper, the New York *World,* had a full-time staff of 1,300 (Mott, *American Journalism* 546–49). The number of weeklies and semiweekly newspapers, which often featured poetry, humorous essays, and short fiction as well as news articles, increased during that same period from 11,200 to 13,100. Americans could subscribe to general magazines guided by editors, such as E. L. Godkin of the *Nation,* who helped shape national political opinion. They could also choose among specialty magazines for almost every hobby. Cyclists, for example, could subscribe to *Velocipedist, American Bicycling Journal, Bicycling World, The Wheelman,* and *The Wheelman's Gazette* at various times between 1870 and 1915. Theatergoers could read about American drama in at least 15 periodicals published in New York, Chicago, Philadelphia, Boston, San Francisco, and Cincinnati (Mott, *History of American Magazines* 260–61). Children and their parents could choose among 60 or more juvenile publications (Bledstein 65–68). Besides these popular magazines, professional trade journals were available that covered engineering, architecture, railroads, airplanes, postal work, crops and irrigation, forestry, and many other fields. Additionally, publishing houses, such as those established by Henry Holt, E. P. Dutton, and Charles Scribner in the 1870s, successfully marketed fiction, children's books, religious books, memoirs and biographies, travel guides, self-teaching books, and medicine and hygiene guides (Tebbel 676–77).

Because of America's industrial revolution of the late nineteenth century, many professionals not involved with publishing also needed superior writing skills. Between 1880 and 1910, the civilian work force in nonagricultural jobs quadrupled, with the highest rates of increase in clerical and managerial positions. During that period, over 200,000 people entered the new civil service (*Historical Statistics* 224, 137–39). With administrative opportunities being created within tiered ranks of managers in trade and manufacturing and with new government jobs being awarded to qualified applicants, new hires would need writing as well as other skills to succeed in their careers.

As the classical education gave way to specialized college majors, students no longer received the earlier required rhetorical training. And the large amounts of material taught in new courses on mining, agriculture, and finance left little time for recitations or writing. But as commerce and publication took on an ever greater prominence and as young people began to enter college to prepare for these careers, the elite few who graduated planned on becoming civic and business leaders. How would these students achieve the high level of skill expected by the public and required by their professions?

2

"The Cry for More English"

As students were completing the new types of college degrees and entering their chosen fields, teachers, business professionals, and the general public voiced concerns about writing quality. College professors criticized the poor composition skills of high school graduates, the inadequate rhetoric and liberal arts training of college graduates—and the results of freshman composition. Business and engineering professionals despaired over the ungrammatical and inexact correspondence of their colleagues. Journalists and their readers continued to censure the irresponsible writing prevalent in many newspapers. In this chapter, we will examine these criticisms as well as some attempts to remedy the deficiencies, attempts that focused on additional writing training that could be offered during the junior or senior year of college.

Blaming the Primary and Secondary Schools

In the early 1800s and before, American students who entered college had been trained by tutors or in private Latin grammar schools that generally offered a seven-year program in mathematics, classical languages, and logic, beginning when boys were between seven and nine. Instruction proceeded by recitation, a method calculated to strengthen the memory; students often memorized pages of conjugations and mathematical rules and then repeated them to the teacher.

Grammar was the first part of the modern discipline of "English" to enter this curriculum, especially after the Revolution, and it gained acceptance by taking on the methodology of foreign language instruction: students memorized and recited grammar rules, studied the parts of speech, "parsed" and diagrammed sentences, and corrected poor syntax, all to foster mental discipline. This prescriptive approach took hold after 1750, with *Murray's Grammar* as the predominant text: from 1795 to 1850 it appeared in 200 editions (Applebee 6–7). By 1819, English grammar study was offered in most American schools; by 1850, the curriculum included more oral drill work, fuller discussions of rules, and some attention to sentence building (Lyman 144). When Hugh Blair became popular at the college level after the publication of *Lectures on Rhetoric and Belles Lettres* in 1783, instruction in perspicuity and precision in style as well as some literature study also entered the secondary school. Older students began to learn literary history from books like Thomas Shaw's *Outlines of English Literature* (1848).

After the Civil War, Matthew Arnold's advocacy of cultural study provided additional impetus for introducing students to literature. In *Culture and Anarchy* (1867), he wrote that literary and historical study could make "reason and the will of God prevail" by "turning a stream of fresh thought upon our stock notions and habits"—to educate and humanize the Philistine middle class. His influential American disciple Horace E. Scudder, a Cambridge school board member and editor of *Atlantic Monthly,* spoke of literature's role in "spiritualizing life, letting light into the mind, inspiring and feeding the higher forces of human nature," and shaping the destiny of America: "Now, in a democracy more signally than under any other form of national organization, it is vitally necessary that there should be an unceasing, unimpeded circulation of the spiritual life of the people . . . in literature, above all, is this spirit enshrined" (Applebee 24; Scudder 31, 33). Complete literary works entered the schools, at first by English and later by

American authors, to emphasize cultural history. They were studied through the historical and philological methodologies then current in college literary instruction, as can be seen in these selections from an 1866 examination on Milton at Cambridge High School:

Give a sketch of Milton's life to 1638.

Give examples of obsolete or obsolescent words from the poems studied.

Give examples of words used by Milton in a different sense than they are today. Illustrate.

Indicate which words in the passage [from "Il Penseroso"] are from the Anglo-Saxon, which from the Latin. How do you tell? (Applebee 29; Witt 169)

By 1870, the new subject matter "English" had come to mean grammar rules and exercises, spelling, vocabulary, English literature, classical literature in translation, oral performance, rhetorical and stylistic principles, and written composition. Private academies and public high schools offered this amalgam as well as courses in modern languages, science, mathematics, history, psychology—and surveying, navigation, and other practical arts—in combinations that varied greatly (Popham 134, 141).

Early evidence of the colleges' displeasure with the writing skills resulting from such fragmented training came in the institution of admissions tests. In 1819, the College of New Jersey (Princeton) mandated that candidates for admission had to be "well acquainted" with English grammar, as did Yale in 1822 (Broome 43). By 1860 most eastern colleges had similar requirements. That year Princeton extended its English testing by asking candidates "to demonstrate not only a knowledge of English grammar but also the ability to write a 'Short and Simple English Composition'" (Wozniak 69). Harvard added a requirement in "reading English aloud" in its catalogue for 1865, expanded and clarified the requirement in 1869–70, and in 1873–74 began testing composition through an essay-length literary analysis:

English Composition. Each candidate will be required to write a short English composition, correct in spelling, punctuation, grammar, and expression, the subject to be taken from such works of standard authors as shall be announced from time to time. The subject for 1874 will be taken from one of the following works: Shakespeare's *Tempest, Julius Caesar,* and *Merchant of Venice;* Goldsmith's *Vicar of Wakefield;* Scott's *Ivanhoe,* and *Lay of the Last Minstrel.* (*Twenty Years of School and College English* 55)

In 1882 at Harvard, each candidate was also given an extra half hour to correct sentences of bad English. At the University of Pennsylvania in the 1880s, entrance exams reflected the skill units in the freshman texts, Abbott's *How to Write Clearly* and McElroy's *System of Punctuation.*

As A. S. Hill described Harvard's exams, their purpose was to alter the high school and elementary curriculum so that the student

> would acquire a taste for good reading, and would insensibly adopt better methods of thought and better forms of expression; that teachers would be led to seek subjects for composition in the books named, subjects far preferable to the vague generalities too often selected, and that they would pay closer attention to errors in elementary matters. ("An Answer to the Cry for More English" 235)

Dean E. W. Gurney's report to President Eliot in 1873 also concentrated on the need for students to leave the lower schools with better basic skills and more knowledge of literature:

> Bad spelling, incorrectness as well as inelegance of expression in writing, ignorance of the simplest rules of punctuation, and almost entire want of familiarity with English literature, are far from rare among young men of eighteen otherwise well prepared to begin their college studies. . . . Now that the College has formally recognized the importance of elementary training in English Composition, and the fact that such training should be given early and in the schools, where alone it can be made thorough, doubtless the excellent instruction in English which is already given in some of our preparatory schools will be furnished in all; and the College can profitably begin the

instruction in this subject as it should do, with rhetoric proper and English literature. (*Forty-Eighth Annual Report of the President of Harvard College, 1872–1873* 48–49)

In 1878, the results of the admissions test confirmed Hill's and Gurney's judgments of the students' reading and writing: 157 of 316 applicants failed the test because of their poor literary knowledge as well as

> utter ignorance of punctuation as to put commas at the end of complete sentences, or between words that no rational being would separate from one another; and a few began sentences with small letters, or began every long word with a capital letter. Many, a larger number than usual, spelled as if starting a spelling reform, each for himself. (Hill, "An Answer to the Cry for More English" 236)

In the *Annual Reports of Harvard College* for the end of the nineteenth century, the president also lamented the students' continuing problems. From 1888–91, 12 to 17 percent were not prepared for admission into English A (*Annual Reports of the President and Treasurer of Harvard College, 1890–91* 75). Noting that the problem was really worse because many special admittance students, who had weaker skills, didn't take the exam, the report urged the lower schools to provide better preparation for the college bound.

Further discontent with students' skills was seen in the appointment in 1891 of a committee of three from outside of Harvard to evaluate English A students. After reading sample themes, the three local businessmen, Francis Adams, E. L. Godkin, and Josiah Quincy, concluded that the students' skills were abominably low: "At one extreme of this class of Freshmen are the illiterate and inarticulate, who cannot distinguish a sentence from a phrase, or spell the simplest words" (Copeland and Rideout 2). Since the preparatory schools were failing, this committee concluded, they should immediately improve their writing instruction—and Harvard should begin increasing its entrance exam standards, excluding those students who could not write. The lower schools were further criticized in an 1895 study of Latin and Greek translations and another in 1897 of freshman composition. The Harvard reports were widely publicized, bringing about a series of reaction articles in newspapers and magazines, an "unprecedented outcry that had made correctness in English a national concern" (Kitzhaber 76).

In 1892, to begin changing the students' preparation, the National Education Association's Committee of Ten, with Harvard's president Charles Eliot among its members, recommended new standards for the high school degree: four year-long "units" in foreign languages, two in mathematics, two or three in English, and one each in history and science. They recommended that literature study, based on the reading lists then used at many eastern colleges, take up 60 percent of the English curriculum and that composition, mainly analysis of literature, take up 30 percent, with the rest of the time devoted to grammar and rhetoric (Russell 65).

The colleges' emphasis on literature study as the route to better reading and writing skills produced radical changes in the lower-school curriculum. Between 1860 and 1900 the number of schools offering courses in grammar fell from 60 to 35 percent, and in rhetoric from 90 to 63 percent. The number of schools offering English literature rose from 30 to 70 percent, with attention given to close analysis along with study of literary forms, literary history, and the authors' lives. The most frequently chosen texts, reflecting the influential college reading lists, were *The Merchant of Venice, Julius Caesar,* the *First Bunker Hill Oration, The Sketchbook, Evangeline, The Vision of Sir Launfal, Snowbound, Macbeth, The Lady of the Lake,* and *Hamlet* (Applebee 34–37).

In 1900, approximately half of the English curriculum was devoted to "composition," but not all of this work really involved writing: only 30 percent of this one-half (or less than one-fifth of the total time) was given to writing, although the numbers were slightly higher for twelfth grade (37 percent of the "composition" half). The rest of the time was given to oral composition, memorization, vocabulary building, the use of dictionaries and encyclopedias, formal grammar and grammar exercises, and spelling (Counts 37). By the 1920s, schools also offered English elective choices, primarily for seniors, in public speaking, business English, journalism, English literature, debate, and other topics.

Although these changes were encouraged by academics who wanted students to obtain similar, thorough training in literature and composition, the fragmented use of "English" time did not insure a high standard of writing skill. As Robert Connors has commented about the Harvard students of the 1870s: "Students failed the Harvard examinations because they had never been asked to do much writing, not because they had failed to grasp their elementary grammar lessons" ("Mechanical Correctness" 66). Reforms of the late nineteenth century, and especially the new emphasis on literature, only lessened the amount of time given to writing. All of the students' writing problems would certainly not be solved through this minimal amount of high school instruction.

The Limitations of What a Freshman Course Could Do

As we saw in the last chapter, the strong reaction to inadequate high school preparation in writing led to a required freshman composition class in colleges. This course, with its attention to grammar rules and exercises, paragraphing, and exposition, was a national tradition by 1910, an attempt to make up for basic skills deficiencies and prepare students for the written work of their majors. But very quickly its originators were displeased with the results and questioned whether the class really helped students or whether it might be a hindrance to their development as writers.

A. S. Hill's freshman text, *Principles of Rhetoric,* was printed in its original and a revised edition 21 times between 1878 and 1898. Following his definition of rhetoric as "the art of efficient communication by language" (iii), this popular text offered basic explanations and rules for each feature of prose. Hill started Book One, "Grammatical Purity," with the following statement: "Grammar, in the widest sense of the word, though readily distinguishable from Rhetoric, is its basis" (1). He first took up good use, barbarisms, and improprieties in the manner of George Campbell and then moved to clearness, force, and elegance of style, giving usage rules along with advice concerning slang, clichés, Latinate terms, etymologies, and tropes. He also included instruction on the four forms of discourse, a much longer section in the second edition than in the first. But by 1887 Hill felt that English A at Harvard had made the students into slavish devotees of forms and rules. He especially criticized their "theme-language":

> I know no language—ancient or modern, civilized or savage—so insufficient for the purposes of language, so dreary and inexpressive, as theme-language in the mass. How two or three hundred young men, who seem to be really alive as they appear in the flesh, can have kept themselves entirely out of their writing, it is impossible to understand—impossible for the instructor who has read these productions by the thousand, or for the graduate who looks at his own compositions ten years after leaving college. ("English in Our Colleges" 511)

To remedy the students' deficiencies, Hill proposed that the department institute new advanced writing courses as either electives or requirements.

Barrett Wendell, whose *English Composition* went through 15 printings between 1891 and 1918, was another one of the first English A instructors. His text also contains explanations of reputable, national, and present usage as well as clearness, force, and elegance of style. Wendell didn't include the four forms of discourse, but he discussed the unity, mass, and coherence of the expository and argumentative essay. In 1909, he still believed in his text: "it seems to me as true as it seemed to begin with; and even my now ripened experience could make nothing much more useful for any who should desire my counsel about the matter it deals with" ("The Study of Expression" 164). But by that time he had stopped teaching freshman composition and was very displeased with its results. He criticized the course for "wasting the very blood of their hearts" ("Of Education" 243) and for being a noble but failed experiment since Harvard students had not improved as writers. Lengthy attention to format and style, he declared, had given the "rules" an immense and misplaced power since "we begin unwittingly to lose the

habit, if we ever had one, of thinking it [the rule] into relation
with other matters," such as audience, tone, and purpose. He
even quoted abstract and passive student prose to show that
rule-based instruction had engendered writing that is "tedi-
ously hard to read":

> I take it that this very lack of appreciation of what we are
> and what we might be is the very fruitful source of both
> mobs and murders and graft in every sphere of our social
> galaxy. . . .
> Though he may not prove in time to be the greatest of
> American authors or the most representative, he certainly
> will hold a prominent place in this epoch of our literary
> history. ("The Study of Expression" 167–72)

Another important spokesman, Fred Newton Scott, head of
the Department of Rhetoric at Michigan, also began to react
against this monolith. His popular freshman text *Paragraph-
Writing,* cowritten with Joseph Denney of Ohio State University, appeared in eight editions from 1891 to 1909. It used
the paragraph as the basis of composition instruction, as "a
unit of discourse developing a single idea . . . like a good
essay, a complete treatment in itself" (Scott and Denney 1).
The book presents familiar features of freshman instruction,
such as unity and coherence and the four forms of discourse,
as represented in paragraphing. In his 1908 book on teaching
and an article from 1917, however, Scott declared that rule-
based standards set by authorities were "untenable, both in
theory and practice," because of the natural fluctuations in
language and the impact of foreign languages, dialects, re-
gions, and the individual (Scott, "Standard of American
Speech" 7). He criticized the "stiff, frigid, and yet inaccurate
style of speech and writing sometimes denominated 'school-
master's English,'" an abstract form that corrupts the child's
natural mental facilities and desire to communicate. For Scott,
one of the worst facets of school English and freshman composition was the continued study "merely of abstract rules and
formulas" (Scott, Carpenter, and Baker 309, 317).
During the 1910s and 1920s, professors from many other
universities enlarged upon these criticisms in articles in the

English Journal. Charles G. Osgood of Princeton argued that students should be taught writing through the content areas, especially through literary study, instead of pursuing a shallow and sterile study of rules. Edward A. Thurber, who had taught at the University of Oregon, satirized the quickly chosen topics used to fill in the blanks of the forms of discourse:

> Sometimes topics are assigned, or rather hurled out of mid-air. These topics have no relation to the student's other studies, but are something extra, which he must cram up upon as quickly as possible and then transport to paper. And the more frequently he writes the better. Let not the sun set upon an unexpressed idea. (10)

He also criticized the course's haphazard combination of readings: "Yesterday the class studied about a steam engine; today it takes up the history of a piece of chalk; tomorrow it is to examine how well a man gives the impression of height of a cathedral" (11). In 1917, Frederick Manchester of the University of Wisconsin declared freshman English to be "a makeshift, a temporary device" causing "a condition of general unsettlement" because it substituted organizations, paragraph rules, and grammar for real self-expression. He hoped that this "Sphinx riddle defying solution" would soon be replaced by "a rationally conceived and thoroughly organized program of education in the mother-tongue" (296–97).

Many critics of the period especially denounced freshman composition's reliance on grammar study and drill. In 1918, Irving E. Outcalt, of the State Normal School in San Diego, wrote that grammar could only profitably be studied as the science of a language, a phenomenon of human development. An empirical study in 1923, by William Asker of the University of Washington, found no meaningful correlation between performance on a grammar test and the ability to correct sentences or write well. Gertrude Buck of Vassar College, who had been a student of Fred Newton Scott, thought that study of sentence constructions apart from meaning should be eliminated from the curriculum:

> Thought which is living, growing, organic in structure, cannot be conveyed or represented by a lifeless, static,

artificial construction. Nor are we studying language by studying such a construction. The sentences which grammar presents to us have in very truth ceased to be language, once they have been cut off from all reference to the various acts of thought-communication which gave rise to them, so that they seem to exist in and for themselves, mere mechanical congeries of words, brought together only to fulfil certain arbitrary requirements of the sentence form as such. (25)

Like Fred Newton Scott, Brander Matthews and G. R. Carpenter of Columbia, and Thomas Lounsbury of Yale, all of whom Buck cited, she recognized that school grammar presented English as though it were Latin—through formal instruction and drill that was of little use to the writer.

These professors could not abolish freshman composition, even at their own universities. But they did call attention to the need for more and better instruction. The "current/traditional" approach, as this class structure has often been labeled, might make a class manageable for a new teacher faced with too little rhetoric training and too many students, but it certainly wasn't the ultimate preparation for the writer—and perhaps no method used in only one course could be. These composition teachers began to look to the junior and senior levels as a place for additional writing instruction that might extend the students' skills and remedy problems caused by freshman composition.

Response from Business and Industry

Impetus for more and better writing instruction came not only from critics of high school and college courses. It also came from business and industry, and especially from professionals reacting to the writing in their own disciplines: to the lack of basic grammatical, stylistic, and organizational skills as well as to the inadequate understanding of audience and purpose, ethical responsibility, and background materials. These critics recognized that an inability to communicate not only produces bad writing, but also leads to bad thinking and to stagnation of the discipline itself.

Response to Technical Writing

In the expanding scientific community, critics responded to the young professionals' inability to communicate complex ideas to various audiences. Engineers had worked hard to foster programs in land-grant and other colleges, envisioning a new generation of leaders, but they found these young graduates to be barely literate—and not even aware of their deficiencies.

Before 1870, there had been few instructional materials on engineering, and thus "technical" curricula contained a large percentage of humanities courses (Connors, "Rise of Technical Writing Instruction" 330). At Michigan Agricultural College, now Michigan State, which opened in 1857, students took English literature in the first year and rhetoric and inductive logic in the second. Their year-long courses also included history, mental philosophy, and political economy. The Florida State College of Agriculture had a professorship of "Agriculture, Horticulture, and Greek," which was held by a master of arts (Eddy 69). Yale hired Thomas Lounsbury, a graduate of Yale College, to train science students in literature and philology (Kirby 105). At MIT, students worked with Professor W. P. Atkinson for two hours a week throughout the four years, first reviewing composition and rhetoric, discussing Duruy's *Histoire des Temps Modernes* and Guizot's *History of Civilization in Europe,* and then considering contemporary issues in politics, economics, and sociology while also writing reports that they read aloud to the class (Mann 38). At Rensselaer Polytechnic Institute, students studied foreign languages, philosophy, history, and law along with physics, mathematics, surveying, botany, chemistry, construction, and mining (Mann 13). In 1944, Joseph N. Le Conte, then 74 years old, recalled the humanistic engineering curriculum offered at Berkeley in 1887:

When I started work in the College of Mechanics, the curriculum was quite different from what we have at present. There were among the prescribed courses, a very rigid course in English covering two years, and the written exercises or 'Themes' were carried on for three years. The study of the German language was prescribed for two years in the

College of Civil Engineering and Mining, and for three
years in the College of Mechanics. (Cheit 62)

After 1870, many vocational educators and other professionals sought to eliminate this large humanities component and
substitute study of the latest technical research. At the Stevens
Institute, founded in 1870, Robert Thurston developed a mechanical engineering curriculum with no general education requirement. At Purdue University, president Emerson White
eliminated Latin and German, fraternities, and membership in
the State Oratorical Society. He hired only vocational teachers,
such as William F. M. Goss, who became chair of the new department of practical mechanics after spending two years oper-
ating a steam engine and two studying mechanics at MIT
(Calvert 49–50). By 1910, the types of engineering courses
had greatly expanded, to include chemical, sanitary, marine, ce-
ment, electrochemical, and others. From 1867 to 1914, the average amount of time spent on humanities study in vocational
programs went from 27 percent to 19 percent. At MIT, for example, the time given to literature, rhetoric, political economy,
and history went from 31 to 18 percent of the curriculum; the
foreign language requirement changed from 31 to 7 credit
hours (Mann 7, 23–24). Within this expanded engineering curriculum, students generally took a standard type of freshman
composition course offered by the department of English or a
division of humanities in the engineering school. They also
took a survey of "the great writers" in the sophomore year.

As the number of practical courses increased, many professionals did not like what they had wrought. Around 1900,
critics began a new opposition, stating that the technical movement had gone too far. With agriculture programs just beginning to gain support from professional organizations like the
National Grange and with business programs just starting up,
the major reaction came from engineers. In 1888, Horace See,
president of the American Society of Mechanical Engineers, expressed concern that the schools were not developing the whole
man but just cramming the memory with vocational details.
Oberlin Smith called for "The Engineer as a Scholar and a Gentleman" in his presidential address in 1890. "Have we not gone

too far in specializing for the undergraduate?" asked John R. Freeman, another ASME president, in a speech at Case School of Applied Science in 1905. "The old academic education fits better for the position where one deals with men, or for the $10,000 position," he declared, "while the technical school fits better for the position that deals with materials, or for the $4,000 position" (64). Alexander C. Humphreys, as Stevens Institute's new president in 1902, dedicated himself to broadening the institute's educational base to include English literature, logic, history, economics, and modern languages (153). Wisconsin's dean of engineering F. E. Turneaure declared in 1905: "The value of a general education as a preparation for law, medicine and theology has long been recognized. As a foundation for the engineer's training it is quite as valuable" (275).

Between 1900 and 1915, engineering pamphlets, journals, and lectures decried the poor writing and thinking skills of engineering school graduates who seemed unable to produce even the simplest reports and letters. When a survey was sent out by University of Michigan students in 1905, the engineers who responded repeatedly pointed to the centrality of writing and to the need for a higher level of expertise: "How few men—engineers and others as well—can write a good business letter" (Breitenbach 4). *The Engineering Record* vilified the current college training: "it is impossible, without giving offence to college authorities, to express one's self adequately on the English productions of the engineering students. . . . Most of them can only be described by the word 'wretched'" (Connors, "Rise of Technical Writing Instruction" 331). H. W. Wiley of the U.S. Department of Agriculture, in a dedicatory address for a new chemical laboratory at the University of Kansas, extended the complaint from engineering to all types of lab science curricula:

I have often been mortified at the English composition of college and even university graduates. Men who have attained eminence in particular branches of study often seem incapable of expressing their thoughts in any proper way. Their English is inexact, clumsy, and inconsequent. Clear expression seems to me to be the legitimate outcome of clear thinking, and the neglect of those early studies which enable one to express himself clearly and forcibly is a fault which can only be remedied by long years of mortification and hard labor. (845)

Henry Carhart, professor emeritus from the University of Michigan, summed up in a university address the many complaints about poor language, thinking, and thus ineffectiveness in the profession:

> The opinion of eminent engineers on the pressing need of a better use of English on the part of members of their profession is the best evidence of the neglect of instruction in English in engineering courses in the past. The acquisition of a clear, terse style is urged by them on the ground that an important feature of the modern engineer's duties is to make reports on various phases of engineering undertakings. These reports are an index of the man, and if they are defective in form or finish, the natural conclusion is that he is also deficient as an engineer. (217)

All of these critics felt that students needed more and better college training in writing, especially in the types of writing they would do in their careers. Their speeches and articles at first did not include suggestions for specific courses or a curriculum, but they did promote the belief that better education was needed not only in mechanical and chemical engineering but also in reading and writing, and especially in the kind of writing inherent to the discipline itself.

Response to Journalism

Another target of both professionals and the public was the current standards of journalism practice. For many Americans, newspapers and magazines provided the only regular contact with the larger world. Just as they depended on these publications, they could be vocal critics of them. Journalists themselves also frequently condemned the standards of their own discipline—especially the content and style of the sensationalized news reporting that became popular in the late nineteenth century.

Towns in America had at first relied on newspapers from England delivered by ship. Leading coffeehouses and taverns imported packets of London papers for their customers. Scotsman John Campbell, Boston's postmaster, began the first continuously published American newspaper in 1704. Its contents, two-thirds of which came from London journals, primarily concerned English politics and European wars. The remainder of the single leaf, printed weekly, had short items on "the arrival of ships, deaths, sermons, political appointments, storms, Indian depredations, privateering and piracies, counterfeiting, fires, accidents, court actions, and so on." By 1765, all but two colonies, Delaware and New Jersey, had daily or weekly newspapers (Mott, *American Journalism* 43, 11–12).

American newspaper printers first demonstrated their capacity to be influential as writers when they mounted bold and effective attacks against English authority during the Revolutionary War. The Stamp Act's repeal was made possible by the newspapers' united opposition to it. This triumph led politicians to begin forming allegiances with editors who might be able to further their causes. Ambrose Serle, supervisor of the Royalist paper in New York, wrote home to Lord Dartmouth in 1776 about this new political power of the press: "One is astonished to see with what avidity they are sought after, and how implicitly they are believed, by the great Bulk of the People. . . . Government may find it expedient, in the Sum of Things, to employ this popular Engine" (Mott, *American Journalism* 107–08). After the war, local and national leaders created their own official organs, often picking the editor, supplying the equipment, and securing monopoly contracts for the publication of government documents and speeches. Noah Webster edited the *Minerva* and *Herald* as mouthpieces for Alexander Hamilton (Emery and Emery 79). Andrew Jackson relied on Amos Kendall, who ran the *Argus of Western America* as a Democratic party organ. John Quincy Adams said of Jackson and Van Buren, "Both . . . have been for twelve years the tool of Amos Kendall, the ruling mind of their dominion" (Emery and Emery 114).

In the 1830s, a new type of paper appeared, the penny daily, that attracted a wider working-class audience with a cheaper price, more lively and local subject matter, and fewer articles on politics. The New York *Sun*, begun in 1833, included police news, society gossip, and human-interest pieces. James Bennett's *Herald* started in 1835 with more local coverage, "theatrical chit-chat," society news, crime reports, attacks on fellow editors, and candid Wall Street reports. The lucrative penny presses quickly spread to other cities, offering a realistic, although sensationalized, view of the contemporary scene (Mott, *American Journalism* 230).

These political and penny papers, with their many articles on local events and their infrequent use of reprints from British papers, helped create the position of investigative reporter. The printing trade still furnished most "journalists," especially at country weeklies and western papers, which frequently reprinted articles from the eastern dailies. A printing business was still a necessary adjunct to any newspaper. But men and women, without training in printing, also began entering newspaper work because they wanted to be writers.

Their sensationalized writing, called "yellow journalism," almost immediately led to a reaction against newspaper writing's purpose and tone. Staunch and influential criticism came from James Fenimore Cooper during 1837–45. In an essay from the beginning of his "war" with the press, he maintained that immoral and ignorant newspaper writers wielded an enormous, malevolent power, that their tyranny extended over "publick men, letters, the arts, the stage, and even over private life" (123):

> The entire nation, in a moral sense, breathes an atmosphere of falsehoods. . . . The dread in which publick men and writers commonly stand of the power of the press to injure them, has permitted the evil to extend so far, that it is scarcely exceeding the bounds of a just alarm, to say that the country cannot much longer exist in safety, under the malign influence that now overshadows it. (121)

During this period, Cooper brought 14 libel suits against various reporters and newspapers, first focusing on the press's ridicule of his suit to gain exclusive right to a picnic ground and then on their responses to his responses. In his *Homeward*

Bound and *Home as Found* of 1838, Cooper fed the fire by creating scathing portrayals of reviewers as amateurs without adequate knowledge of literature and without any standards for judgment; *Home as Found* was then declared to be "absolutely beneath criticism" by James Webb, editor of the New York *Courier and Enquirer*. Hundreds of reporters and editors carried on the war, writing columns through which they vented personal animosities but also debated the appropriate style and content of newspaper writing (Mott, *American Journalism* 308–09).

In 1840, as this debate raged, New York journalists attacked James Gordon Bennett's penny paper, the *Herald*, for its emphasis on sex and crime and for its slanderous personal attacks. The *Evening Star, Courier and Enquirer*, and *Evening Signal* called for a boycott and labeled Bennett an "obscene vagabond," a "polluted wretch," and a "venemous reptile" (Mott, *American Journalism* 237). Personal hatreds led to physical violence, which Bennett sensationalized through further editorials:

> As I was leisurely pursuing my business yesterday, in Wall Street, collecting the information which is daily disseminated in the *Herald*, James Watson Webb [editor of the *Courier and Enquirer*] came up to me, on the northern side of the street—said something which I could not hear distinctly, then pushed me down the stone steps, leading to one of the broker's offices, and commenced fighting with a species of brutal and demoniac desperation characteristic of a fury. (Nevins 118)

When papers around the east coast carried on this fight, the *Herald* lost a third of its circulation and Bennett promised to change his ways. This extended melee led to further reactions against unethical reporters, such as that by Lambert Wilmer, a long-time newspaperman, in *Our Press Gang* in 1859:

> I charge the newspaper press of America with invading the sanctuary of private life, disturbing the peace of families, giving extensive circulation to groundless and malicious slanders, calumniating the worthiest and most honorable men and the purest and most innocent women, driving

many objects of its detraction to phrenzy and desperation, and making them in reality as vile and worthless as they are represented to be by the malignant and remorseless slanderers. (52)

Although these critics were focusing on current and past newspaper policies, they recognized that the only hope for real reform lay in the future: in better education for writers and editors. Lambert Wilmer, for example, linked dishonest journalism to poor education:

Five per cent. of them, perhaps, are men of good education and superior abilities. Ten per cent. of them, it may be, are men of common sense and common-school education. Fifty per cent. of them, at least, are men *without* common sense and with no education at all—certainly with no education of that kind that would qualify them to become public instructors. (65–66)

Some critics also condemned the lower-school education of journalists, stating that the scattered attention to prose provided no preparation for writing accurately and ethically. A few newspaper editors, like Whitelaw Reid of the *New York Tribune,* also began to focus on altering college education to develop "a professional esprit de corps that will discourage the habit of perpetual personal attacks upon individual editors rather than upon the newspapers they conduct and the principles they advocate" (Lee 8). Like engineering leaders, these writers did not delineate a specific curriculum—as chapter 7 indicates, the beginnings of college journalism instruction involved much disagreement and experimentation—but they did feel that some advanced training would be requisite for improving the standards of their discipline.

By the end of the nineteenth century, criticism of the preparation for writers was coming from almost every quarter. Lower-school teachers complained that the increasing numbers of students prohibited them from teaching writing frequently or well. In their large classes, they had to deal with "basic skills" like grammar, spelling, and vocabulary, with literature, and with everything else that could be labeled "English." College administrators blamed the lower schools for poor skill levels, but didn't offer a workable model for reform. College instructors often repeated the high school teachers' lack of success. Many of them began attacking the new freshman composition courses as misguided or inadequate; a semester or year certainly didn't seem to be enough. Industry and journalism professionals echoed their concerns; in frequent journal articles and speeches, they maintained that students should have been leaving the lower schools—and certainly college—with better writing skills. With high school and freshman writing curricula becoming institutionalized, the only place to go for more or better writing instruction was to the advanced level. The first suggestions for advanced curricula were broad and optimistic— that one or more new courses might teach specific genres and a sense of professional responsibility while also correcting basic writing deficiencies as well as the mistakes of earlier teachers. College professors would have the difficult job of crafting the specific offerings that could fulfill these purposes.

3

At Harvard and Beyond: Advanced Composition as a Composite Course

As freshman composition became codified as basic, required work, many professors and business people decided that such a class could not successfully complete the students' training, that to enter professional disciplines and become writers, students would need more than the limited composition experience of the lower schools and the two college semesters of grammar, paragraphing, and forms of discourse. For these critics, the specialized course work of the last two college years involved too little writing to make up for remaining deficiencies. In 1879, for example, A. S. Hill complained of the inattention to writing quality at the upper division: "the professor, absorbed in a specialty, contented himself with requiring at recitations and examinations knowledge of the subject-matter, however ill-digested and ill-expressed" ("An Answer to the Cry" 234). Like other teachers, he recognized that juniors and seniors were doing less written work as larger class sizes, new textbook materials, and lab sessions changed the college class structure. Faculty concerned with research, graduate teaching, and professional training had, as David R. Russell has stated, "a license to complain about poor student writing but an institutionally sanctioned excuse for not devoting time to their undergraduates' writing" (63).

More writing training than that given to freshmen in composition classes and to upper-division students in courses within their majors seemed necessary to critics like Hill. But what type of instruction would be an appropriate part of the students' practical and diversified education? Could any type answer the complaints about students' skill levels and professional writing standards? What would a teacher do if given just one semester in a busy curriculum? How would the teacher deal with the varying goals and abilities of the students?

The first answer came from Harvard: general "advanced composition" classes where students could work on different genres to develop their own interests and strengths, remedy their deficiencies, and prepare for their careers. While Harvard professors created English A, B, C, D and then restructured English A as the sole requirement, A. S. Hill and Barrett Wendell experimented with this model of advanced composition as an elective, a chance to enact their criticisms of freshman composition. They intended these advanced courses not as more review of the four forms of discourse, paragraph rules, and grammar, but as advanced work that would introduce students to new voices, subjects, genres, and audiences. In these classes, Hill and Wendell could establish a workshop setting and foster collegial relationships among writers, and thus encourage students to approach their work as professionals.

A. S. Hill taught the first year-long advanced elective course, English 5, in 1877 to 20 seniors and 11 juniors. To enter the class, students had to submit a writing sample and an explanation of their reasons for seeking advanced training. Hill designed this class, he wrote in 1887, to teach his students to "put forth naturally and with the force of their individuality." He especially wanted them to get away from an abstract school voice or "theme-language." Hill structured his class sessions to evoke a more natural prose: he allowed students to develop their own topics in daily 10-minute in-class sessions, an experiment that he found "unexpectedly successful":

Having no time to be affected, they are simple and natural. Theme-language, which still haunts too many of their longer essays, rarely creeps into the ten-minute papers. Free from faults of one kind or another these papers are not; but the faults are such as would be committed in conversation or in familiar correspondence. The great point has been gained that the writers, as a rule, forget themselves in what they are saying; and the time will come, it is to be hoped, when they will be correct as well as fluent, and will unite clearness in thought with compactness in expression, and vigor with well-bred ease. ("English in Our Colleges" 512)

Besides these short papers, students wrote longer essays once a fortnight, either on assigned topics or topics of their own choosing. The class functioned as a workshop:

Three hours a week are spent in criticism of the themes in the presence of the class, criticism in which all take part, and which now and then leads to animated discussion. Often the best themes present the most matter for comment; and some of the best as well as some of the worst writers make great improvement in recasting their essays after they have been criticised. ("An Answer to the Cry" 239)

According to Hill's teaching notebook, he used the following topics in 1877–78 for the 12 longer assignments: what I have read in English literature, a story for a five-year-old child, a comparison of an Austen and an Edgeworth novel, a topic of the student's choice, "relics of barbarism" at Harvard, proposed improvements of Harvard's class day, Sunday hours for the library, a synopsis of chapters from Hill's *Principles of Rhetoric,* a topic of the student's own choosing, a topic drawn from Burke's speeches on America, the American poet and poem whose reputation the student thought would live longest, and the bigotry of unbelief or a topic of the student's own choosing or participation in a debate. During each subsequent year, through 1883–84, Hill varied the topics completely for the 12–16 papers, but the students always wrote on at least one literary subject, such as whether knowledge of Homer in the original would have helped or hindered Scott or Keats, how Homer and Shakespeare handled Thersites' character, and what message *Idylls of the King* portrayed. Two or three times each year, Hill also assigned topics concerning Harvard, such as how well the college prepared students for business, whether public opinion existed at Harvard and who made it, whether there was too much drunkenness at commencement—and whether English 5 could be improved. Students also wrote on moral questions such as the propriety of signed and unsigned newspaper articles, excessive devotion to objects, and man's duty not to despair, and on political and social topics such as President Arthur's view of the civil service, the status of the two political parties, and the drawbacks of being an educated man in America, an important question at a time when college education was still viewed as impractical and elitist. Each year, students could write on two or three topics of their own choosing, perhaps trying out creative genres like the fable or modern story, and they could submit alternative ideas for other assignments. Hill also gave a midterm exam concerning literary and political topics and a final consisting of literary analysis.

In his teaching notebook, Hill commented on the success or failure of some of his topics. When he asked students to write on whether this country should have a literary class, a topic of perhaps great importance to him at a time when business and government were expanding rapidly with little regard for the advice of eastern academics, he found that the question was "half understood." Of the quotation "The sure way to make a foolish ambassador is to bring him up to it," he commented, "no one wrote on it." The topic of liberty as an enemy to ideas he judged as "poor." He found the art of giving and the synopsis of *Principles of Rhetoric* to be "pretty good" and "good"; the sincerity of Byron and poetry versus prose seemed "good" and "tolerably good" (Lecture Notes from English 5).

In shaping a course around literary, social, and political subjects, Hill was reflecting his own experience and interests. A Harvard graduate from 1853, Hill obtained an LL.B. from the law school at Harvard in 1855. Although he was admitted to the bar in New York, he worked as a law reporter and then as a contributor to *North American Review, Atlantic Monthly, Putnam's Magazine, Harper's Magazine,* and other journals. Some of his articles concerned authors such as Charles Lamb, Jonathan Swift, and Laurence Sterne, but he also wrote on French,

English, and American politics—on Greeley's writings on the Civil War, the impeachment attempt against Andrew Johnson, the Republican convention of 1868, French communes—as well as on humorous themes such as puns and punsters. In 1872, ill health caused him to leave journalism and begin a career at Harvard. While teaching there, he wrote six textbooks, including *Principles of Rhetoric* and the more basic *Foundations of Rhetoric,* as well as essays about teaching writing, but he also continued to write journalistic pieces, such as two articles on cattle ranching in Canada for the English publication *National Review* in 1883. Although Hill wrote freshman textbooks, he did not shape the course around college formats and grammar but instead chose a variety of subjects and encouraged his students to let their content shape their organization and style, as students in English A did not.

Another advanced class instituted by Hill in 1878–79, English 6, stemmed from the debates that served as a choice for a final assignment in English 5. So that students could prepare adequately, he announced the political, historical, or literary questions a fortnight before the class meeting, which would last three hours to give ample time for the debate. Two students opened the argument on each side and one on each closed it, with the opening speakers having 10 minutes and the closing speakers having 15 minutes. Between the opening and closing speeches, nearly an hour was given to volunteers on either side, each being allowed five minutes only. In the remaining hour, instructor and students made comments on "points of manner as well as of matter, to the way of putting things as much as to the things put." In 1879, Hill described the detailed criticism that went on in the class:

> Awkward attitudes, ungrammatical or obscure sentences, provincial or vulgar locutions, fanciful analogies, far-fetched illustrations, ingenious sophisms, pettifogging subtleties, ineffective arrangement—all come in for animadversion; and corresponding merits for praise. ("An Answer to the Cry" 239)

By 1884–85, Barrett Wendell also taught English 5. Like Hill, he required a page or more of writing each day on a topic of the student's own choosing, although he generally had students do this writing outside of class, and longer themes on a variety of topics, with the opportunity provided for them to write fiction as well as nonfiction. A student critic read each long paper and wrote a page or more about it; these critiques were discussed in class workshops and individual conferences; then students had an opportunity to revise before finally submitting their papers to Wendell. About lectures on textbook chapters, then a central part of English A, Wendell commented: "the use of text-books, as distinguished from personal instruction, is reduced to a minimum" ("English at Harvard" 132).

Wendell's responses to the longer papers show that, like Hill, he expected students to support their ideas fully and use language effectively. In his marginalia, he treats students as members of a writing community to which he also belonged, as advanced writers getting opinions from a more experienced colleague. In 1885, William Morton Fullerton, an 1886 graduate, wrote a paper in which he used Mill's *Essay on Liberty* as a starting point for a harangue against socialistic agitation and changes in the Harvard curriculum, both evidence of the "wide-spread unfaith of the time." (He did recognize that each generation felt nostalgia for the morality of earlier periods: "Some one in 1985, no doubt, will be speaking of our own age in exactly similar terms.") At the end of the paper, Wendell wrote this personal reaction to the student's purpose and style:

> Full of suggestion; but in spite of it's [sic] length not quite clear. You arraign liberty; but show us nothing better, as far as I can see. Would you have us all sign the 39 articles?
>
> I cannot too warmly express my delight in the earnest exuberance of your style; but more & more I grow to think that you are in great danger of losing yourself in the rapidity of your movement. Do you always know where you are going? Do you quite get anywhere? —This note I make in haste. It is ill expressed; but shadows at least a real feeling. Your Pegasus needs a tight rein.

With other papers, Wendell continued commenting on the student's wordiness: "Your style lacks terseness. Make that quality your aim for a while." About a long fable involving fireflies,

hornbugs, flying glowworms, and fairies in the English coun-
tryside, Wendell offered this comment, again showing his relationship to the student as a fellow writer:

> As your critic says this is full of charm—a charm which I
> feel even today, when I am conscious of being in a hate-
> fully unsympathetic mood. It is this mood, I suppose,—&,
> to go a step further back, a deplorably good dinner which
> I ate last evening,—that impels me to say one or two hate-
> ful things. In the first place, then, I think you surround
> your fable with too much comment, etc. Your introduction
> is too long. And it is not only too long for the fable, but
> also too long for what is in it; it is diluted. Then your style,
> particularly in that part of your work, has a somewhat
> forced vivacity. There is too much exclamation, too many
> "dear readers", etc. Finally, I think you would have done
> better frankly to lay your scene in our own country, to
> sketch with that nice sympathetic power of yours some
> scene that you know well. I am not an entomologist; but I
> have an idea that the glow-worm of England crawls; that it
> is wingless. Of course such a criticism as this is grossly
> unasthetic [*sic*]; if not positively illiterate. Still, it comes
> into my head. If you read "Emilia" [Wendell's poorly re-
> ceived Gothic romance], by the way, you will have a chance
> to return it with interest.
>   To sum up my impression of this theme in a sentence—it
> is so common that I cannot suppress a constant disappoint-
> ment that it has not the final charm of apparent simplicity.

Fullerton's other papers included an analysis of Blaine and
Cleveland as presidential candidates, a paper on Thackeray as a
humorist, one on biography writing, and a short story. Wendell
continually pushed him, through blunt but personal comments,
to reach further in developing his ideas and in shaping his style
for a reader (Fullerton).

Like Hill, Wendell reflected his own writing interests in his
teaching, as one of his students commented: "Barrett Wendell
was expressing once more the artist in him" (Eaton 450). He
had graduated in 1877 from Harvard, where he helped found
the *Harvard Lampoon* and created its central character, Hollis

Alworthy—a stereotype of the "dapper, sophisticated, superficial Harvard aristocrat" (Self 32). Wendell entered Harvard's law school the next year, but failed the bar exam in 1880. Hill, who had been his professor, offered him a position as theme reader that year. He became an assistant professor in 1888 although he faced opposition because he lacked a graduate degree in English. He wrote two Gothic novels, *The Duchess Emilia* (1885) and *Rankell's Remains* (1887), as well as *Ralegh in Guiana* (1902), poetry and drama "in the Elizabethan manner." He also wrote pieces on Harvard's social and intellectual life, on Puritans and the Salem witch trials, and on French and American politics as well as book reviews and essays on writers such as John Greenleaf Whittier and Francis Parkman for *Lippincott's, Scribner's,* and the *North American Review.* Wendell's work was often poorly reviewed, and his colleagues acted disdainful of his creative efforts, a response that Wendell found disheartening: "it is maddening to have to do one's best work in an amateurish way, if not actually on the sly—at the risk of having fingers pointed at you if you are found out" (Self 34).

In both his literature and writing classes, Wendell offered students the opportunity to pursue creative projects and receive supportive responses. In his courses in medieval and Elizabethan drama, students could choose to write imitations of the play forms being studied. Wendell also encouraged them to write additional plays so that they might be prepared to participate in the professional theatre, the development of which he forecast in *A Literary History:* "if a dramatist of commanding power should arise in this country, he might find ready more than a few of the conditions from which lasting dramatic literatures have flashed into being" (518). Like Hill, he envisioned advanced composition as being devoted not to textbook study or college formats but to experience with professional forms like the short story and newspaper article, frequently in projects of the students' own choosing.

By 1892, LeBaron Russell Briggs, an English professor and dean of arts and sciences, also taught English 5, treating the students, many of whom were in the graduate program, as though he were training them to be journalists, reviewers, poets, and short story writers. He assigned daily themes and then allowed students to pursue their own longer writing projects, mainly creative writing. Like Wendell, he had students prepare for workshop sessions by writing one-page analyses of their classmates' work. His student and biographer, Rollo Brown, described this English 5 class experience, which resembled what students also encountered with Hill and Wendell:

> The actual operation of the course was so simple that it seemed not to be based upon any theory at all. The members ranged in age from twenty or twenty-one to forty or forty-five, although most of them were in the middle or late twenties. They came from Maine, New York, Ohio, Kansas, Texas, California—men of all mental attitudes, but most of them with a little of the divine terror in their eyes. They brought novels half completed—sometimes a man brought two or three; they brought volumes of unpublished verse; they brought essays on the times; they brought shadowy outlines of "the great American" novel; they brought sometimes only a vague but persistent feeling that they must write.
>
> These men were asked to submit something immediately. The Dean began "dipping into" these themes at once; he was as eager as a boy at Christmas to see what he had. And then after that first, somewhat preliminary theme, something substantial must come in as often as once a fortnight. It might be a section of a novel; an essay; a short story; a sonnet sequence; a group of three or four lyrics. Opportunity was at hand. If the muse had been calling—or even whispering—no one now had an excuse for refusing to follow.
>
> When these contributions came in, they were not turned over to some competent assistant for reading and correcting; every one of them was read by Dean Briggs himself— and commented upon in red ink! A freshman with a bent for the statistical method once computed that Dean Briggs had written enough comment on other men's work to fill more volumes than H. G. Wells had written. And most of it, he believed, was infinitely more interesting.

Twice a week the thirty men and their leader met together for an hour of criticism. He read from the work he had examined, called for discussion of it, sometimes discussed it with great earnestness or fascinating subtlety himself, and then asked the men to write at once, before they left the room, a criticism of what he had read; sometimes, of the classroom discussion. At the next meeting he read some of this criticism—he had carefully corrected it in the intervening days—and some of the longer, more pretentious themes. Occasionally, in the course of the hour, personal alignments and schools of criticism began to appear. The Dean then shrewdly refrained from having further oral criticism until a variety of new themes had broken up the too definite alignments. A man could not so easily tell who was criticizing his work when the criticism was in writing, there flat on the desk under the Dean's kindly scrutinizing eye. Besides, the effort to identify criticism wholly from "internal evidence" was an exhilarating exercise in style. The course and the minds of the men in it must be kept mobile.

For most men, the essence of the course was concentrated in the conferences, which, through some magic, the Dean·always found time for. Slipped down in one of the chairs by the long table in his office, he went casually through the themes a man had written, and talked with intimate earnestness about structure and good taste and stylistic detail. Sometimes a young novelist who had come with a suitcase full of stories, hoping at last to find an appreciator of his genius, talked pleasantly with the Dean for a half-hour, and then, without telling him that he had ever written stories, decided in the secrecy of his own heart to burn everything he had written and begin all over again. Sometimes a country youth from some more or less rural college, after having long feared that he should never be able to find good story material, discovered here in twenty minutes that he had lived all his life in a region made of the stuff of romance. Sometimes a young poet gained the impression that he was already on the way, and needed most of all a hardy self-discipline. (71–74)

In this demanding atmosphere, many students began their professional writing careers. Louis F. Ranlett, who had served in World War I in France and returned to the states when he was wounded, first worked for a magazine, *The Youth's Companion*, as a librarian from 1915 to 1917, and then entered Harvard. He took English 5 with Briggs during 1920–21. As his class work, Ranlett wrote editorials, a one-act play, translations of French literature, book reviews, short stories, poetry, and a war novel that he turned in chapter by chapter. During the year, he sold several of his stories and poems to *The Christian Endeavor World*, *The American Legion Weekly*, and *The Youth's Companion*, which then had the largest magazine circulation (Bledstein 68). He stapled to the front of each piece a list of possible places to send it. In his class folder, he also included his letters of acceptance and rejection.

Briggs's detailed comments on the papers demonstrate his concern for this writer's development. He read the poems closely, criticizing, for example, a line that described the wind sweeping past the narrator since in the next line he leapt to meet it. In a later draft of this poem, entitled "Winter Night," the wind "assails" the narrator instead of sweeping by. In a poem called "To Certain Doubters," Briggs objected to the line "The inward, tingling joy that showed me God," writing in the margin that "tingling," which he also circled in the text, "possibly lacks dignity in this context." He also criticized "did feel" as a weak verb form. His comments, such as this one concerning a description of a mountain scene, showed that Briggs considered his students as young professionals: "For anything so hard to do, this is exceptionally good. It is spirited, rarely if ever turgid, and in only two or three places marred by those hard-worked descriptive phrases that a *writer* can scarcely avoid" (emphasis added) (Ranlett). In an interview session 21 years later for an alumni report, Ranlett commented that he remembered Ethics A and English 5 most clearly of the courses he took at Harvard because "both encouraged thinking" (*Harvard Class of 1921* 602). After college, he combined careers as librarian and writer, publishing articles and two novels, although not his war novel from English 5.

In 1884–85, Barrett Wendell introduced a second advanced composition course, English 12, which became one of the most popular of Harvard's electives (Morison 75). It frequently enrolled 200 students, whom Wendell would split into seven sections. In this course, as in English 5, Wendell drew from his own experiences as a novelist and journalist, attracting many talented students who wanted to explore a variety of genres, share their efforts with a class, and submit their work to a demanding critic/teacher. In this class, he gave students more freedom to pursue their own topics, to experiment with various creative genres. According to Walter Eaton, one of Wendell's students who became a drama critic for the *New York Tribune* and a Princeton professor of playwriting, "What Wendell did for Harvard was actually to make a place there—for a time, at least—in which the artist could find encouragement and counsel" (450). W. E. B. DuBois also enrolled in English 12, believing, as he wrote in a theme for Wendell, "foolishly perhaps, but sincerely, that I have something to say to the world, and I have taken English 12 in order to say it well" (39). (He recalled in his 1940 autobiography, "Barrett Wendell rather liked that last sentence. He read it out to the class" (39).) Robert Frost entered Harvard to study with William James and attempted to bypass freshman English, "hoping that he was qualified to take Barrett Wendell's course in advanced composition" (Thompson and Winnick 104). Robert Herrick, later a novelist, University of Chicago professor, and author of books on teaching English, wrote that Wendell "has had a greater influence upon the craftsmanship of the writer than any other American man of letters" (7). Besides providing a writing community in class, Wendell sponsored the *Harvard Monthly* so that his students, such as George Santayana and Frank Norris, could reach a larger audience, and he helped many of them, including Santayana and Edwin Arlington Robinson, to find their first publishers. About the widening influence emanating from Wendell and from Briggs, Rollo Brown wrote:

But when some one sits down to explain why in the early years of the twentieth century the younger readers and

writers of America began to concern themselves with
something less hollow, less conventionally formed than
much of the literature conventionally styled "New England," he cannot leave Briggs and Wendell out of consideration. They trained men to look at the world with their
own eyes, and to write directly and honestly about what
they saw, without regard for the traditional ways of looking at things. The men thus trained went all over the country to teach in the colleges and universities, and they
carried with them the gospel that the world right where
one lives is interesting if one will only look and think. And
the students whom these men in turn trained went away
from college by the thousands—and later by the tens of
thousands—to find joy in the same unaffected experience.
Only the blind can say that this fact has had nothing to do
with our attempt, more or less national, to develop a literary art directly from the soil. (59)

In English 12, as in English 5, Wendell required that a page
of work be written each day and be turned in before 10 A.M.
Students chose their own topics for their "daily themes," but
Wendell recommended that they write on current occurrences.
Each year, as his teaching notebook indicates, he began the
class by discussing the value of these daily themes for achieving
a regularity of habit, gaining the power to hold attention,
learning an efficient style, cultivating the power of observation, and correcting habitual errors (Notes of Lectures in English 12). He especially wanted students to see the possible
writing material all around them and to improve their descriptive powers: "What I bid them chiefly try for is that each
record shall tell something that makes the day on which it is
made different from the day before" with the result that "each
new bundle of these daily notes that I take up proves a fresh
whiff of real human life." He felt that the writer who "gives a
material body to some reality which till that moment was im-
material, executes, all unconscious of the power for which divine is none too grand a word, a lasting act of creative
imagination" (Self 133). Throughout the term, he read daily
themes aloud to provide examples of the students' strengths

and weaknesses. He commented in his notebook for October 8, 1885: "Then read two or three dailies, showing vicious tendencies of style; & two or three others showing the direct simplicity of style that should be aimed at in this course." On November 10, he used sample dailies to discuss the students' writing tendencies: "cheap lines, careless looseness—each sentence tacked with *&*, fine writing, confusion, careless rambling, clear criticism, some good themes" (Notes of Lectures in English 12).

Taking the class in 1886–87, Thomas Clyde, an 1888 graduate, wrote daily themes about college football, races, theatricals, his washerwoman, a newspaper he had worked for, the class day officers, a walk around Fresh Pond with friends, and his dismay over a late final exam that would delay his salmon fishing. Wendell wrote short comments on the back of each folded theme, usually describing the subject and the style. Concerning one on the new policy of voluntary attendance at chapel, he wrote, "Subject—good, style—easy." About one concerning the variety of handwritings: "Conventional or trite subject, style—negative." Clyde often tried out symbolic description:

As I was passing through the yard yesterday I met the last straw hat of the season. I stopped and gazed at it sadly. How lonely and out of place did this emblem of summer seem, amid the fallen leaves and keen winds of autumn. There it sat on its owners [*sic*] head like some crippled bird that can not flee at the approach of winter and seek a new summer in the south, but sits miserable and alone and shines as the chill fall breezes ruffle its plumage.

About this theme, Wendell commented, "Straw hat forced." In another daily theme, Clyde wrote about a mountain walk:

By the time we rached [*sic*] Mount Auburn it was quite dark, and a fog that was coming in hung over the white tombstones making them appear more mysterious and ghastly than usual. The scene was a very appropriate one for ghost stories; and my friend, who had a good stock of them, told some excellent ones.

On the back—"Walk. Vague" (Clyde).

Cyril Herbert Burdett also took the course in 1886–87. Wendell frequently marked Burdett's papers with "prolix," encouraging this student to curb his wordiness. About local politics, Burdett wrote, "The election of a United States senator in Massachusettes next January promises to be most interesting. Already the fight has begun in the newspapers and is now waxing hot," and Wendell commented, "conventional subject; style diffuse." When the student said about studying Hobbes's *The Leviathan* in Philosophy 14 that "surely no greater bugbear could be forced upon a man than the thought of being compelled to read that work," he had finally earned the comment "some ease." In another daily theme, Burdett recorded the difficulty of daily journal writing:

> I have exceedingly hard work to select subjects for my daily themes. I get my pen and paper and then sit and scratch my head. What have I done to-day that is worthy of record. Let me see, got up eight o'clock, breakfast 8:20, prayers 8:45, library at 9; lecture at 10, examination in Phil 4 at 11 lunch at 12:30 and so on. Did I see anything in all these places about which I can write one page. Well I saw a great many things but when you come to write, you want a subject possessing dignity or importance. Most things you see are very common place; a description of them would be so terrible stale. No it is very much out of place to think of it. So I sit and think and think, and the longer I think the harder it is to find anything. If I only could keep the fact in mind that I was on the lookout for subjects and could catch the casual points on the fly and treasured them up for future use it would be all right but what with lecture, examinations, reading, and the thousand and one things a man has to do, this thing is liable to escape him. But at the end of ten minutes I get disgusted and take the weather as a subject and write —— about it or when there is anything in that line I fall back on the questions "ever new and ever fresh" politics. A subject must come anyway and somebody or something has to suffer for it.

Wendell also judged this entry favorably, as "colloquial" (Burdett).

In William Bayard de Billier's work of the same year, Wendell found more to praise. He wrote "vivid and readable" on a daily theme connecting fine arts lectures with campus tastes:

> Men I pass day after day have a most peculiar mode of dressing themselves. Here, see this man—so long and thin that, as Oliver Wendell Holmes says, he looks as though he is split and dried. Covering this manly form is a blue coat, from the collar of which, as he swaggers along with his chin high in the air, peeps out the brightest of red cravats.

De Billier's daily theme about going to the library to work on a forensic ("Upon entering the door I stopped for a moment to glance around and was struck by the marked stillness everywhere; the only sound being caused by the shutting of a drawer or dropping of a book") merited "rather effective" (de Billier). These short notes helped Wendell prepare for his class discussions, and they provided succinct feedback for the writer.

In addition to these page-long themes, students submitted longer fortnightly themes, poems, and stories, which Wendell's class presentations helped them to plan and revise. In 1885–86, as his teaching notebook indicates, students did a short article or story on a current topic for the first "fortnightly" and a piece of fiction or nonfiction based on ideas from the works of Macaulay for the second. While students worked on these projects, Wendell talked about clear style, word use, and paragraphing as well as the "positive virtue of cleanup in writing." The third fortnightly, in November, could be anything "of a literary character—a criticism, or an original work of belles lettres." In class, Wendell discussed how to use an author as a point of departure. In answer to student requests, he also lectured on point of view in narrative. The fourth theme, in early December, was a description of something the students had actually seen; as preparation Wendell lectured on descriptive technique. That month, he commented in his teaching notebook, "On the whole I am satisfied with the men, & not with myself. I am tired out." In 1886–87, when he commented "beginning this year with a health & strength that last year I despaired of," the first longer theme or story was to concern social life at Harvard, a topic Wendell chose because he was writing an essay on it. In the second half of the year, he wanted students to pick one general subject, "subdivided out into as many facts as there are themes" (Notes of Lectures in English 12).

After five years, in 1889, LeBaron Russell Briggs and Arlo Bates from MIT also taught English 12, in multiple sections during most terms. By 1898, John Gardiner, who wrote for *Nation* and *School Review,* had joined this group. By 1908, Charles Townsend Copeland, a literary biographer and Carlyle scholar, was the main instructor. To enter the class, prospective students had to submit a 600-word account of their previous writing training, their coursework for that year, and their purpose for taking English 12, as well as other samples of their work. On his syllabus, John Gardiner stated that he accepted only men "with some native equipment" and with "promise of showing this special capacity" as a writer. One student from 1919, senior William Gaston, felt that he should not have to undergo this process because he had written an article, concerning Oliver Goldsmith as an army man, that had been published. When he submitted this piece for a second review, he wrote on the back of it: "Despite its vagarities and solecisms, the 'Chicago Tribune' accepted this—why can't you?"

Under these new teachers, English 12 still involved detailed criticism given in workshops and conferences. John Gardiner made this professional level of group involvement clear in his first-day handouts: "In general, the purpose of such a course as English 12 is analogous to that of an atelier—to turn out men with something like a *professional* command of the art in which they are to practise" (emphasis added). In mentioning the artist's studio or *atelier,* Gardiner was referring to a French artistic tradition of the nineteenth century, of informal academies, *ateliers libres,* where avant-garde artists worked together and with a mentor who provided them with models and with ongoing criticism, but with little formal instruction.

Like the other new teachers, Charles Townsend Copeland continued the earlier English 12 combination of assigned and free-choice topics in several genres intended to prepare students to be writers. One of his first assignments was an imitation of Edwin March Wheelwright's comic dialogues. On a dialogue by Charles M. Storey, a senior, Copeland noted, "you give nothing of the pungent drollery of Wheelwright at his best . . . only the husks" (Storey). Walter D. Edmonds, a 1926 graduate, wrote 300-word translations from French poetry and a play every two weeks. He also turned in an editorial on Harvard examinations (returned to him with the comment "rewrite completely with great zeal") and a book review as well as several short stories. On one longer story, of 20 pages, Copeland's comment shows his desire to make students aware of the quality level they would have to reach to succeed as writers: "I suppose such writing won't get you far as a *professional author* in America or England; but, from time to time, as an interlude among sterner labors, I should think this sort of work might be a refreshment" (emphasis added) (Edmonds). One of Copeland's students, Harry T. Baker, who became a creative writing teacher at Goucher College, praised this focus on professional standards and on the world beyond college that remained part of English 12 after Hill and Wendell:

> Each student in a course in advanced English composition should be allowed to write what he can do best, allowed to develop his special talent or talents. He should not be forced to write elaborate papers for, say, English 15, which may be Arthurian romance or the plays of Shakespeare, but should be encouraged to write something of the sort that professional writers actually do turn out for publication. Harvard University, which offers no courses in journalism, has long been famous for having two or three such inspiring teachers of advanced composition as Professor Copeland and Dean Briggs, who, instead of being "outside human nature," as an acid critic has expressed it, are very much in touch with human nature and with the shifting panorama of Boston, as well as that of the Harvard "Yard," and of New York or Chicago as well as Boston. Such teachers are citizens of the world. They hate pedantry and love the human appeal. They are humanists. (38–39)

In 1889, Harvard also instituted a separate advanced elective course in argumentation, English 18, first taught by George Pierce Baker. In this class, students wrote forensic essays of generally 15 pages. Among the topics in 1889–1890 were whether home rule should be granted to Ireland and what part Robespierre played in the French Revolution. One student's title page lists a rhetorical situation for an essay concerning the effects of English commercial policy on the colonies: "Delivered to an audience of Englishmen a few years before the Revolution by a colonist" (Swan). Class handouts indicate that students learned the form of an extended brief: an introduction, expository discussion of the steps of the case and its special issues, argumentative proof organized by headings, refutation, and a conclusion where the special issues would be settled and the proposition affirmed or denied (Leaflets on English Courses). By 1900, the course had been renamed The Forms of Public Address.

In 1882, Harvard also added English 22, Sophomore Composition, taught by Lewis Edwards Gates. In this class, students found another chance to develop their own creative writing projects and work closely with the instructor. Frank Norris received criticism in English 22 on his published short stories and on early manuscripts of *McTeague* and *Vandover and the Brute;* he especially worked with Gates on effective description and the objective voice. He described this class as a writing workshop for the 300 students:

> The literary student at Cambridge has but little to do with lectures, almost nothing at all with textbooks. He is sent away from the lecture room and told to look about him and think a little. Each day he writes a theme, a page if necessary, a single line of a dozen words if he likes; anything, so it is original, something he has seen or thought, not read of, not picked up at second hand. Once every two weeks he writes a longer theme, and during the last six weeks of the year, a still longer one, in six weekly instalments. Not a single suggestion is offered as to subject. The result of the system is a keenness of interest that draws three hundred men to the course and that fills the benches at every session of the class. The classroom work consists merely in the reading, by the instructor, of the best work done, together with his few critical comments upon it by the instructor in charge. The character of the

themes produced under this system is of such a high order that it is not rare to come across one of them in the pages of the first-class magazines of the day. (Walker 93–94)

In the classrooms of Hill, Wendell, Copeland, Briggs, Gardiner, Gates, and others, Harvard provided a model for a workshop approach to advanced composition. At other colleges, especially along the east coast, such as Amherst, Colgate, Columbia, Hamilton, and the University of Pennsylvania, English departments began to offer advanced classes that involved daily themes and longer assignments, individual attention, and a chance to experiment with a variety of genres. From 1880 to 1890, only seven eastern colleges had this type of elective. By 1920, however, 29 of 37 eastern colleges offered these advanced courses. Although some schools like Columbia, Dartmouth, and Harvard introduced an array of choices, many had only one course above the freshman level, but the trend was toward two or more by 1920 (Wozniak 129–32).

The University of Chicago, which opened in 1893, immediately instituted advanced courses under the guidance of Robert Herrick, who had been one of Barrett Wendell's students before serving as an instructor of rhetoric at MIT from 1890 to 1893 and then going to Chicago. In its first year, Chicago offered three quarters of composition for freshmen as well as elective courses in "advanced composition and investigation of Rhetorical problems" (University of Chicago, Catalogue 1893 73). Herrick taught English 5, Advanced English Composition, using Wendell's *English Composition* and requiring daily themes and six long essays during the two-quarter course. In the first term, students heard lectures on style and discussed their written work in class; in the second, they studied a variety of genres including fiction, history, exposition, argumentation, and criticism. As Wendell had done, Herrick requested that students write their six themes or stories on one subject, perhaps selected from another course. Herrick also taught English 6, Advanced English Composition, a one-quarter course involving daily themes and longer essays, lectures on the development of English prose, and work with the students' style. The department also offered English 3, Argumentative

Composition, and English 4, Oral Debates, similar to Harvard's English 18 and English 6.

At Hamilton, a Seminar for Writing English, in which students criticized freshman themes as one of their ongoing assignments, served a select few. At Princeton, an elective entitled Advanced Composition was open only to seniors who could profit from the work and were qualified to do it. In this course, students could choose to write personal essays, arguments, drama, or verse. As Professor Charles G. Osgood commented, these advanced students were ready to pursue independent projects:

> At this point, under pressure of lively feeling and opinion from within, with a definite notion of what he wishes to do, and enough desire to make him patient in practice, the student will have learned, and does learn, about writing what he might in his shallower and more sterile days have wasted precious time over, without learning it particularly well, and to the neglect of more pressing matters. (235)

At Bowdoin College, an advanced course called Literary Composition involved the collaboration of six professors, each presenting one subdivision: translation, essay, oration, short story, drama, or verse. At the end of the course, all instructors and students met to critique the writing (Bowdoin College, Catalogue 1915–16 166–70). At Dartmouth in 1920, Practical Composition covered book reviews, editorials, articles, essays, and business correspondence. Dartmouth also offered Advanced Practical Composition, an intensive course in writing articles, essays, and criticism (Dartmouth College, Catalogue 1920–21 39–40). As two 1939–40 course descriptions show, the Harvard model continued to influence instruction in subsequent decades:

> Advanced Composition. The writing of miscellaneous "assignments," representing current forms of literary experimentation, such as essays, stories, and verse; submitting these to an audience of classmates and instructors for criticism. Approximately one completed piece of work is called for each week. Open to juniors and seniors whose applications have been approved by the instructor. Three

hours weekly, for one or both semesters. (Union College, Catalogue 1939–40 34)

Advanced Composition. Writing and class criticism of weekly papers. Admission restricted to those who have submitted a satisfactory sample paper to the instructor before June 1. Specific assignments in widely varied materials and methods of writing. Revision and rewriting. (Williams College, Catalogue 1939–40 110)

Although these classes testify to the influence of Harvard teachers like Hill, Wendell, Briggs, and Copeland, their course model—involving motivated students in a workshop setting—could not always be replicated at other schools. Most colleges recognized that students needed more work with composition than could be provided by the freshman course, but some concentrated their efforts on the least prepared students instead of the best. And the teachers might be emphasizing literary or linguistic study in their own careers and thus not be prepared to deal with the creative and journalistic forms encouraged by Wendell and Hill. As the idea of a second level of instruction spread, the advanced course often came to resemble not Harvard's English 5 and 12, but more freshman composition for juniors and seniors—the four forms of discourse, correctness, and lectures.

Mount Holyoke had one of the largest complements of advanced current/traditional offerings, elective courses entitled Descriptive Writing, Narrative Writing, Advanced Exposition, and Advanced Argumentation (Mount Holyoke College, Catalogue 1910–11 47–48). In 1909 at Penn State, Advanced Rhetoric, a sophomore course, covered grammatical purity, diction, structure of sentences and paragraphs, and essay forms, with Berkeley's *A College Course in Writing from Models* as the textbook (Pennsylvania State College, Catalogue 1909–10 214). By 1911, the department also offered an advanced course on argumentation and two advanced courses on exposition (Catalogue 1911–12 239). In 1910, the University of Kansas offered advanced courses entitled Narration, Description, Exposition, and Argument (University of Kansas, Catalogue 1910–11 147–51).

Teachers of these advanced classes in 1900 or 1920 often relied on their own materials or a freshman text, such as those by Genung, Hill, Wendell, Carpenter, Pearson, and Scott and Denney, all weighted toward formats and correctness. One of the few texts designed for advanced college students, Harry Robbins and Roscoe Parker's *Advanced Exposition,* published in 1933, reprinted in 1935, and released in a second edition in 1940, extended the freshman model for an advanced audience. The authors begin by recognizing the difficulty of finding a text designed for the advanced course, which, they say, was offered "in every college" (vii). The book covers the modes of exposition, but it also deals with other more practical and difficult forms: abstracts, precis, translation, technical exposition, criticism, and scientific, didactic, and aphoristic essays. Although this text clearly follows the paradigm that dominated the freshman course, Robbins and Parker tried to meet the needs of a more advanced group by stating the principles behind the modes, including sophisticated readings, and discussing additional formats used by professional writers.

Beginning in the 1950s, the new Conference on College Composition and Communication worked at defining advanced composition and its "aims, texts, and methods," as their report was subtitled in 1958, because the proliferation of advanced and remedial, open and structured classes made the label unclear. From 1954 to 1971, ten invitational workshops at the March conferences focused on this task. Some panelists felt that the course needed to have remedial goals, to reinforce the lessons from freshman composition as students entered their majors. Others insisted that "advanced" composition should extend the skills of the very best writers. In 1958, the group found many variations within existing offerings: fairly large required courses with a heterogeneous group as well as small classes of dedicated writers; lectures, group work, and conferences; texts ranging from rhetorics to readers to current magazines to the teacher's notes; open-ended assignments as well as structured sequences of expository modes. The group could only agree that the course was "gaining ground": "It is now being required of more and more students. Schools that have not offered it are planning to do so" ("The Advanced

Course" 165–67). While this workshop simply noted the diversity, the 1963 group reacted to it vehemently:

> We don't agree as to what Advanced Composition should be or is. We all do different things, which are all good, but none of it seems to make any difference. Most students can't write when they enter college, and write worse when they leave, having inflated their vocabularies merely. We do not agree about the objectives of the course, the content, the order of topics, the number or length of essays, the emphasis various factors in composition should get, or what related materials to bring in. ("The Undergraduate Advanced Composition Course" 190)

After declaring that they all planned to go on teaching advanced composition, "whatever that is," the group adjourned to the Statler-Hilton bar.

In 1966–67, the CCCC decided to get serious about a definition for advanced composition by creating an invitational workshop whose job it would be to decide on guidelines. Designated by Richard Braddock, chaired by Richard Lloyd-Jones, and with Francis Christensen among its members, the group met at two CCCC conventions and corresponded in between. Like the earlier committees, they recognized that the course should not be remediation, that it should "represent substantial progress beyond the goal of the local freshman course." The course, they asserted, should concern the students' writing, not models from readers; it should focus on the writing process; and it should be taught by well-trained professionals, teachers who thought of rhetoric and writing as their research interests. Their most specific curricular advice was that the course should cover "the range of the freshman course but in greater depth" ("Guidelines and Directions" 266).

In each decade, colleges continued to offer two or three of these advanced composition courses, to provide remediation for students who needed more freshman composition or a challenging arena for young professionals—or an unwieldy combination of the two. At some schools, these courses were requirements for education, English, or business students, but they generally remained as electives taught by literature professors or instructors, rarely by teachers who considered rhetoric, journalism, or creative writing to be their academic specialty.

Since our notion of advanced education implies a narrowing, an immersion into one specific field, this general type of advanced writing instruction never found a secure niche. For upper-division writing instruction to flourish, it would have to be designed by specialists who could gear it to one student population and to one type of writing. Advanced composition, in the hands of Barrett Wendell and many others, has been a challenging course, great because of its lack of precise definition, because it can be shaped and reshaped by individual students and classes and teachers. But that lack has caused it never to be firmly institutionalized: the general advanced composition course did not become the primary paradigm for advanced college writing instruction.

4

The First Specialized
Courses and Course
Arrays

As universities grew and added new professional curricula, a "general" approach to advanced composition no longer seemed sufficient. The possible clientele for an advanced writing class was becoming more diverse, perhaps impossibly diverse since teachers would have to serve students in English, history, business, engineering, agriculture, nursing, and other majors, whose abilities could range from lowest to highest. General courses could provide these students with basic skills, but they could not provide the professional orientation and specialized guidance that might be expected from advanced college instruction.

Soon after Harvard and other schools instituted advanced courses, writing teachers began to participate in the professionalizing and segmenting of education: to serve new student constituencies and departments and, thus, at a time when the liberal arts found themselves on the defensive, to provide English departments with their own marketable "real world" courses. Like agriculture, engineering, home economics, and other fields, writing began to be viewed as sets of skills to master in college and apply in specific careers. Teachers thus began to approach writing through its professional manifestations, primarily as creative writing, magazine and newspaper writing,

61

business writing, and technical writing. Each decade brought more courses covering more specialized segments of professional writing, taught along with the one or two general advanced composition classes.

This writing instruction was an American, not a European, development. British academics continued to maintain that creative writing could not be taught because the artistic gift is not teachable. Individualized guidance on technique, which might be helpful to those few with the gift, would not be an appropriate part of the general undergraduate experience. Perhaps because British and continental universities could rely on the personal instruction and assignments of their tutorial system and on the work of their graduate programs to introduce students to academic and professional discourse, they also did not perceive a need for the journalism and technical writing classes that began to enter American colleges along with courses on poetry and fiction.

In American English departments after 1900, especially along the east coast, writing courses concerning specific genres developed quickly. Before 1900, most east coast schools had only general advanced writing classes: Lafayette College, for example, had no advanced composition courses, Hamilton College offered general intermediate composition, New York University had intermediate and advanced composition and an advanced argumentation course, and Mount Holyoke College offered advanced composition and argumentation. Between 1900 and 1910, Lafayette still had no advanced courses, but Hamilton added technique of the drama, New York University introduced advanced composition and newspaper writing, and Mount Holyoke added sophomore English, journalism, principles of structure, principles of style, structure of the novel and drama, and pedagogy of rhetoric. To supplement their general advanced offerings, these schools and others were adding creative writing, journalism, and instruction on teaching, additions with which English professors probably felt the most comfortable and which reflected the needs of their liberal arts students.

In the next decades, the new classes included more general advanced offerings as well as business and technical writing and specialized courses in creative writing and journalism. Between 1910 and 1920, Lafayette added a course on the short story and one on English for engineers. New York University added business English and advanced composition while Hamilton and Mount Holyoke kept the same offerings. During 1920–30, Lafayette added advanced composition, creative writing, feature writing, and newspaper reporting, Hamilton added sophomore and senior composition, New York University kept the same offerings, and Mount Holyoke added magazine writing and beginning and advanced courses in the short story. Between 1920 and 1940, these schools instituted more courses in creative writing, journalism, and business and technical writing, including book editing, writing for motion pictures, and report writing (Wozniak 260-305).

This increase in specialized writing courses was not confined to the east. Because of their commitment to professional education and their openness to innovation, the new land-grant schools across the country instituted even larger numbers of courses following the same emphases—on creative writing, journalism, and business and technical writing. Course offerings at the University of Michigan are the best known from this time period, but other schools developed similar course arrays.

At Michigan, the commitment to rhetoric and composition came primarily from Fred Newton Scott. In the 1890s in the English department, Scott, a Michigan Ph.D., offered essay writing, advanced composition, the science of rhetoric, and the development of rhetorical theory. At that time, his colleague Alfred Hennequin was conducting classes in play writing that had begun in the late 1880s (Kinne 87). By 1908, in a separate rhetoric department formed in 1903, Scott and his colleagues, including Joseph Thomas, who left in 1909 to develop the rhetoric department at the University of Minnesota, had instituted several general advanced composition courses following the forms-of-discourse approach to instruction: one covering description and narration and one on exposition and argument, and a more advanced class on the theory and practice of argumentation. An additional seminar resembled Wendell's English 12: "a limited number of advanced students who write with facility and are in the habit of writing" submitted their manuscripts for correction by the class and also studied principles of criticism and revision.

Scott also designed specialized professional education in writing for undergraduate and graduate students. For English students planning to be teachers, he offered a course on teaching composition and rhetoric. An additional two-semester graduate seminar in rhetoric and criticism concerned a different subject each year, such as "the origins of prose; the nature and origin of the leading types of discourse; the psychology of figures of speech; the rhythm of prose; the sociological basis of the principles of usage; the origin, development, and laws of the process of communication." For creative writers, Scott introduced a course in short story writing. Prospective journalists might take review writing, a course designed "to give practice, under direction, in the writing of book-reviews for newspapers and magazines," and one on newspaper writing, a seminar involving theory as well as the editing and publishing of "several numbers of a daily paper" (University of Michigan, Catalogue 1909–10 126–28). By 1920, the department had added new courses in all these areas: a seminar on rhetoric and criticism for doctoral students; play writing; newspaper practice; a seminar on newspaper problems; newspaper feature writing; editorial writing; a seminar on editorial practice; and advertisement writing (Catalogue 1920–21 346–51). For an alumni newsletter, Scott's colleague Louis A. Strauss commented on the knowledge and drive that Scott brought to these new offerings:

> Professor Scott was the ideal teacher of the science and art of literary expression. His range of interests was well-nigh universal. An acute critic, an accomplished linguist, a skillful bibliographer, he had at command, beside his spendid [*sic*] background in English literature and his thorough mastery of the history of rhetoric, a wide knowledge of the arts of painting and music and of many literatures, ancient and modern, a profound grasp of philosophy in general and aesthetics in particular, and such an appreciation of many sciences as few teachers of the humanities possess. His seminary in the History of Rhetoric was as fundamental and vital in the equipment of a teacher of English as any

graduate course I have ever known. . . . Dr. Scott's conception of rhetoric was catholic in the extreme; it was limited only by the range of his own personal interests, which really means that it was not limited at all. Under the spell of his magnetic and stimulating personality his students developed to their utmost capacity. They are to be found everywhere—brilliant teachers, successful writers, and men in every walk of life upon whose tastes and characters his influence is indelibly stamped; and they are not backward in saying so. (332)

Besides these individual classes, Scott developed a complete curriculum in journalism with newspaper writing as the first course. In 1909, the university offered a program of study in journalism, which included the one journalism course, credit for work on student or university publications, and other course work in rhetoric and the humanities. A faculty committee designed a specific course of study for each student. By 1920, a more structured curriculum contained 18 hours of journalism, 12 hours of other rhetoric offerings, 10 hours in the English department, and courses in foreign languages, history, and political science.

At Michigan, other academic units also began to offer writing courses after 1900. In that year, the engineering program required two semesters of freshman composition and French or German; seven hours of engineering or humanities electives were the only other nonscientific requirements. By 1910, however, the college had become more aware of the importance of professional writing. Within the engineering college's separate department of English, Abraham Strauss and his colleagues offered courses on scientific literature, commercial correspondence, technical journalism, technical exposition, and contracts (University of Michigan, Catalogue 1909–10 243; Russell 122). The Bachelor of Engineering required one of these courses; a Bachelor of Science in Engineering, which had a larger liberal arts component, required all of these one- or two-hour classes. In 1910, the university also had combined undergraduate and graduate programs in nursing and law that required two upper-division classes on the forms of discourse as well as freshman composition. The undergraduate program in business required no advanced writing instruction, but by 1920 students could elect to take two classes on business writing, covering advertising, commercial correspondence, and sales, that were offered by the rhetoric department.

Other universities, led by teachers with less rhetorical training than Scott, did not develop as many classes on linguistics and theory but did begin to offer various types of professional writing. In the English department of the University of Chicago, besides the counterparts of Harvard's English 5 and 12, Robert Herrick and his colleagues developed a course on writing short stories and historical monographs; one on writing literary criticism, in which students studied works by Chicago faculty and by Wilhelm Scherer, Matthew Arnold, and James Russell Lowell to learn the "practical art of criticising"; and a seminar on the history of rhetoric (University of Chicago, Catalogue 1893–94 72–74). By 1896, the department had added a course in rhetoric and composition for teachers, in which the students wrote each day and studied textbooks, teaching methods, and theme criticism; two courses in reading and writing short stories; and a course on poetry writing, in which students studied Milton, Tennyson, and Lowell, practiced "metrical composition," and participated in "mutual criticism." These courses were taught by Herrick as well as William Wilkinson, Edwin H. Lewis, author of an 1894 study of the English paragraph that had been his dissertation, and Robert Lovett, like Herrick a student of Wendell's at Harvard (Catalogue 1896–97 70–73). Lewis also offered business writing and business journalism as extension courses.

Chicago first offered a journalism program in 1899 as one track within the new College of Commerce and Administration, which also had tracks in banking, transportation, and trade and industry. To give students a sufficient liberal arts and social sciences background, the journalism program required them to study political economy, European and English history, sociology, and municipal government, with professors from those departments, as well as the development and organization of the press. Instead of taking advanced writing courses, the students submitted their writing each term to professors from the English department. By 1910, English 5, advanced composition, was also a requirement for students entering the program.

At the University of Wisconsin, a "who's who" list of writing teachers and textbook authors developed similar types of advanced courses. The sophomore composition course, a college requirement in the 1890s, focused on the four forms of discourse and on readings: "The writing of essays in description, narration, argumentation, and exposition proceeds with the study of brief extracts of literary masterpieces. Milton and Macaulay, Addison and DeQuincey, Ruskin and Huxley, are critically studied for diction, adaptation, and mastery of materials" (Frankenburger 136). This class, as well as freshman composition, was guided by William B. Cairns, a Wisconsin Ph.D. who began teaching in the English department in 1893. His influential texts, *The Forms of Discourse* (1896) and *Introduction to Rhetoric* (1899), provided the instructional materials and models for emphasizing forms of discourse in freshman composition and the advanced courses. Edwin Woolley, a graduate of Chicago who came to Wisconsin in 1909 after completing a Ph.D. at Columbia, created the exercises needed to emphasize mechanical correctness at both levels. His *Handbook of Composition*, destined to become one of the most widely used textbooks in the country, appeared in 1907 with the apt subtitle: "a compendium of rules regarding good English, grammar, sentence structure, paragraphing, manuscript arrangement, punctuation, spelling, essay writing, and letter writing." He also published *Mechanics of Writing* (1909), *Exercises in English* (1911), and *Written English* (1915).

The first course in newspaper writing at Wisconsin began in 1905, with a class of 30 students. The teacher was Willard Bleyer, who worked as a journalist from 1892 to 1898, received a Ph.D. from Wisconsin in 1904, and became an assistant professor of English there in 1905. That course became the nucleus of the four-year "Courses Preparatory to Journalism," which appeared in the Wisconsin catalogue in 1906; of the four-year course in journalism outlined in 1909; and of the five-year School of Journalism established in 1927. Bleyer administered the English department's journalism program from the beginning; he became assistant professor of journalism in 1909 and later dean of the journalism school. His popular texts reveal the increasing specialization of journalism courses at Wisconsin and elsewhere: *Newspaper Writing and Editing* (1913), *Types of News Writing* (1916), and *How to Write Special Feature Articles* (1919). Bleyer's staff included Grant Milnor Hyde, who in 1921 published journalism's equivalent to Woolley's handbook: a *Handbook for Newspaper Workers* "treating grammar, punctuation, English, diction, journalistic structure, typographical style, accuracy, headlines, proofreading, copyreading, type, cuts." Hyde also wrote three other journalism texts: *Newspaper Reporting and Correspondence* (1912), *Newspaper Editing* (1915), and *A Course in Journalistic Writing* (1922).

In 1905, assistant professor Edward Hall Gardner led Wisconsin's English department into another field of specialized writing. He taught the university's first business writing course that year, an elective taken by students from many different disciplines. His text, *Effective Business Letters* (1915), reflects the course's concentration on letters, memos, and correct grammar. As a professor of business administration, he later taught classes and published books on marketing, collection methods, dictation, and the economics of advertising.

In 1910 in Wisconsin's College of Engineering, freshmen took a specialized composition course emphasizing the modes of discourse, with stress on technical description and exposition. One advanced elective offered further practical training in informative writing. Another had a humanities emphasis, with readings geared to helping students see the relationship of science to society (University of Wisconsin, Catalogue 1900–01 112–13; Catalogue 1910–11 140–41). The latter course was taught by Karl Young of the English department, a Michigan undergraduate who studied with Fred Newton Scott and did graduate work at Harvard. After he came to Wisconsin in 1908, he established his reputation as a scholar with *Origin and Development of the Story of Troilus and Criseyde*. He also published several writing texts and class anthologies: *Century Readings for a Course in English Literature* (1910), *Essays for College Men: Education, Science, and Art* (1913), *Freshman English: A Manual* (1914), and the *Students' Handbook of the Facts of English*

Literature (1910). Young's approach to technical writing influenced other teachers, like Frank Aydelotte at MIT, who wanted students to understand the moral questions involved in scientific pursuits.

Between 1900 and 1910, many other schools began supplementing freshman and general advanced composition courses with specialized offerings geared to their own students and faculty. The University of Kansas began to offer journalism courses. The University of Florida offered journalism as well as industrial journalism for its engineering majors. Louisiana State University established journalism courses and then a journalism department. Iowa instituted classes in poetry and short story writing. Illinois brought in several business writing teachers and also offered journalism. The University of Pennsylvania offered advanced composition in the English department and newspaper practice in the school of commerce. Texas A&M had an advanced composition course required of juniors in agriculture and an advanced argumentation course required of juniors in engineering; students in the two-year course covering textile engineering took a sophomore course in expository and argumentative prose and business correspondence. The University of Minnesota began technical writing and other advanced courses under the guidance of Joseph Thomas.

These rapid developments did not always meet with assent in English departments. Literature teachers saw their colleagues developing different, perhaps not as intellectual, interests and taking students away from Chaucer and Shakespeare. The new classes involved allegiances, often strained at best, with teachers from engineering and business. They also entailed substantial knowledge of professional discourses with which most English teachers were not familiar. These beginnings would not be a harbinger of a fully developed writing curriculum within the English department. As we will see in subsequent chapters, specialized writing courses were only held together in the same department by the same teachers for a very brief time: these new classes almost immediately became part of different academic units. Beyond a listing of these first attempts is the distinct history of each type of advanced course.

5

Teaching Creative Writing

In Harvard's English 5 and 12, Barrett Wendell and his associates allowed students to write poetry and short stories, giving them detailed criticism of their work and information on publishing. Other schools also offered such opportunities within their general advanced classes. As writing instruction became specialized, however, separate creative writing courses on the short story, versification, and play writing appeared at east coast schools and elsewhere, along with journalism and business writing. Although these early creative writing courses, taught between 1890 and 1915, did not have the impact that New York and Europe, back porches, and bookstores had on that generation of writers, they did establish an American college tradition, a course type and teaching method unknown in Europe. In the 1920s and after, creative writing classes, enriched by elements from off-campus groups, would provide a primary training ground for American writers, and a place for many other students to learn about language and meaning.

Creation of an American Course

Drama, poetry, and fiction writing courses, like other versions of advanced composition, developed in American colleges after

70

1890 along with the belief that modern universities could and should teach everything, preparing students for almost every type of profession. Paul Engle of the University of Iowa's writing program has acknowledged creative writing's connection to other new fields:

> The astonishing flexibility of approach and subject matter is the American university's contribution to education. If there is an activity of man which is useful or attractive, let us study it. With that attitude, it was easy to fit creative writing into a university curriculum. (*Teaching Creative Writing* 27)

Creative writing may have been recognized as an academic specialty because its practitioners could earn a living by 1900: thus it was at least somewhat like engineering, agriculture, and other modern university disciplines. Publications burgeoned in the 1880s in this country. In 1885, only four general monthly magazines could boast of circulations of 100,000 or more, with a combined readership of 600,000; in 1905, the 20 general magazines had a combined circulation of over five and a half million. As magazines also developed that concerned political and social movements, the arts, schools of philosophy, trade and industry, and hobbies, the total number of American periodicals increased by more than a thousand in just five years, between 1885 and 1890. During this time there was also a dramatic increase in the amount of fiction published in magazines—stories reprinted from anthologies, commissioned from established writers, and accepted from beginners, as well as novels appearing as serials. *Collier's* offered serial novels, fiction, poetry, and humor writing as well as articles on women's issues, theater, and sports. *McClure's* published Kipling's *Kim* in serial, stories by Willa Cather, Jack London, O. Henry, and Alice Brown, and poems by A. E. Housman and William Butler Yeats. *Century* paid $50,000 for a serialized life of Lincoln; *McClure's* paid $25,000 for *Kim*. Literary magazines like the *10 Story Book* and the *Wayside Monthly* offered prizes to encourage new writers. *Argosy*, which featured adventure, mystery, and action stories, published early works by James Branch Cabell, O. Henry, Susan Glaspell, and Upton Sinclair. In 1900, the *New York Times* estimated that 20,000 Americans considered themselves to be professional writers although the majority were "either not successful or only apparently so" (Mott, *History of American Magazines* 4–11, 38–41). Most writers certainly did not receive the same pay as Kipling—the going rate for beginners varied between half a cent per word and a cent per word—but magazine publication possibilities had multiplied, an adequate living could be made, and article writing might lead to book-length projects.

Changes that specialization brought throughout the college curriculum also fostered the teaching of creative writing. As freshman and advanced composition began to concentrate on forms of expository discourse, students could less frequently find outlets for creative writing in those classes. As students took fewer Latin courses, which involved imitations and translations of poetry, they lost another forum for their writing. Also, as all teachers became responsible for larger numbers of students and classes and as they offered fewer tutorial sessions, students had less opportunity to pursue independent projects.

Teachers such as Hill, Wendell, and Fred Newton Scott realized that freshman composition at best offered very limited training, and at worst caused students to become more restricted in their thinking and more pretentious in their style. Creative writing could free and engage students, enabling them to play with words and meanings instead of constantly attending to restrictive forms of discourse and grammar rules. These teachers also recognized that creative writing instruction could create better readers. In the preface to his 1917 text *Verse Writing,* William Carruth stated that the goals of poetry writing courses were an increase "in control of a prose style and in general appreciation of the niceties of language," development of "esthetic taste, of intellectual judgment, and of spiritual sensitiveness," and "preparation for keener appreciation of poetry" (2–4).

Behind this emphasis on freeing students, engaging them in their own experience, and encouraging them to learn about a discipline by working in it lies the influence of John Dewey and other educational reformers. Dewey came to the University of Michigan as a teacher of philosophy in 1884 and there published

"The Ethics of Democracy"; he went to the University of Chicago in 1894. By 1903 professors comprising the "Chicago school" of pragmatic instrumentalism emphasized the crucial role of self-expression and active experiential learning in education. High schools and colleges began to endorse the personal topics and first-hand descriptions as well as the peer workshops used in creative writing courses because they seemed to embody Dewey's theories. "The setting for a class in creative writing should provide an atmosphere in which the student can believe that his own thoughts and his own experiences and his own feelings are intensely real and are as important as anything he might read out of a book," wrote the Deweyan Lawrence H. Conrad of the New Jersey State Teachers College at Montclair for the Commission on the Secondary School Curriculum in 1937 (23). In a 1934 study of creative writing instruction, Burges Johnson of Syracuse University argued that the word "creative," and the creative writing instruction that had become a unit of most high school English classes and an elective at most colleges, had entered education along with Dewey's term "progressive" (*Creative Writing* 3).

From its beginnings, creative writing instruction was beset by contradictions stemming from these varied audiences and goals: a curriculum created to enliven the writing of overly taught sophomores or to create better readers and learners might not provide the best instruction for serious writing students. Such students would need more, but would work on techniques help them to write originally? Could genius be taught or even coached? Many young writers felt that academia had little to offer them. Many academics felt that little could or should be offered beyond literature and other liberal arts courses.

The First Courses and Texts

Whatever the doubts and contradictions, many schools instituted creative writing courses around 1900. By 1910, for example, courses on versification were taught at Fordham, Middlebury, Iowa, and Missouri, on the short story at Chicago, Michigan, Nebraska, and Wesleyan, and on play writing at Pennsylvania, Hamilton, and Harvard, with Iowa, Illinois, Chicago, and Michigan offering several courses on different genres. Academics who published fiction or poetry, but who were primarily teachers and scholars of literature, usually taught these classes. Perhaps 10–15 percent of American colleges offered at least one creative writing course before World War I: others offered students the option of doing creative projects within advanced composition workshops or literature courses.

Before 1920, a higher percentage of women's colleges offered creative writing instruction than men's, because education in the arts seemed like a more appropriate component of a woman's education. Between 1900 and 1910, Mount Holyoke introduced courses on structure of the novel and drama and verse composition. Newcomb College in New Orleans began a short story writing course in 1908 with emphasis on literary appreciation, historical development of the genre, and writing techniques. Tulane, the affiliated men's school, did not offer creative writing until 1939. When Edna St. Vincent Millay took writing courses at Barnard in 1913 to prepare for college admission, her teacher, William T. Brewster, a Dryden and Carlyle scholar who had written a freshman composition text and was then translating Lope de Vega's *New Art of Writing Plays,* helped her to revise her story "Barbara on the Beach," which was published in 1914 (Brittin 5).

College-level creative writing textbooks, many by teachers who had taken advanced writing courses at Harvard and Chicago, began appearing by the end of the century. In the 1898 text *Short Story Writing,* Charles Raymond Barrett, who as a Chicago undergraduate had studied short story writing with Edwin H. Lewis, discusses titles, character types, story structure, and the quest for a publisher. He uses examples from American short stories, most frequently those of Hawthorne and Poe, and from manuscripts by his own students. In *The Art of the Short Story* (1913), Carl H. Grabo—an instructor at the University of Chicago who mentions in the preface his debt to his colleague Robert M. Lovett, who had been a student of Wendell's at Harvard—also covers character types and story structure. In *Short Stories in the Making* (1914), Robert Wilson Neal, who had received master's degrees at both Harvard and Yale, had written for newspapers, and was teaching at

Massachusetts State College, discusses the short story as a drama in narrative, with action set in time and a distinct crisis, much like a one-act play. All of these books teach formats: they provide instruction and examples for stories emphasizing setting, action, character, or theme, assignments that could create a course syllabus.

Early poetry writing texts also concentrate on form. In *Verse Writing* (1917), William Herbert Carruth, an 1893 Harvard Ph.D. who first taught at Kansas and went to Stanford in 1897, provides information on poetic vocabulary, poetic license, and the high calling of the poet, as well as exercises like the following. Fifteen of these paired assignments, which involved writing and critical reading, were suggested as a semester's work:

> Write two pieces of four stanzas each, iambic tetrameters, with masculine endings (same as Exercise I) but with rhymes *a: a, b: b* (couplets), the one on The Trees of the Santa Clara Valley, The Engineer, or My Dearest Hope; the other on an optional theme. Report some poems in this measure, noting their tone, whether light or somber, romantic, reflective, or didactic. . . .
>
> Write two pieces of twenty lines each in iambic pentameters, rhymed couplets or alternating rhymes, one on California Wild Flowers, True Religion, or War and Peace; the other on your own theme. Try in either the effect of "run-on" lines, *i.e.* of carrying a clause over from one line into the next. Report some familiar verse in this measure. (64, 76)

This text provides short professional examples after each assignment and an additional section of student samples reproduced along with the teacher's comments concerning them. For a poetry writing course, Carruth recommends that students purchase this book as well as a manual on versification, a rhyming dictionary or a thesaurus, and several poetry anthologies (57–58).

Although these texts concentrate on formats and on professional prose, they also offer help with what might now be called prewriting or planning. In *Writing the Short-Story* (1908), J. Berg Esenwein discusses observation, experience, self-study, reflection, reading, discussion, and note taking. In *The Art of the Short Story,* Carl Grabo helps students with generating ideas for stories that emphasize theme, plot, or character:

> Suppose, however, my story has its inception in character. Here, again, the idea may spring from specific observation or from the unaided imagination. If observation, the creative process may be this: in Smith, my neighbor, I am struck by an extreme conscientiousness. He performs his every duty with painstaking thoroughness. There are other qualities in Smith which, for my purposes, are irrelevant. He is rather forgetful, and has neglected to repay the three dollars he once borrowed of me; and I, knowing his sensitiveness, will never remind him. For my story Smith is a man with one dominant quality, conscientiousness. I then conceive a man resembling Smith, but freed of his forgetfulness and other distracting traits. Him I place in a situation which will try him to the utmost, reveal the full potentialities of his character in the one direction. It may be that life has never tried the real Smith in such fashion. In my story, therefore, I present my creation with a conflict of choices, let us say one of love and duty. (200–01)

These books also examine the decisions that writers make as they plan and draft so that the final product will portray their intended emphasis:

> Stevenson writes of *Treasure Island* that he deliberately made his pirates not realistic and true persons, but pirates as a boy conceives the breed, fierce mustachioed fellows, with wide trousers and belts full of pistols. In *Treasure Island* character is not the objective. Provided the buccaneers walk and fight with sufficient swagger, it is enough; the rest is soul-stirring adventure. Less skillful writers think nothing of checking the flow of action to bore and disconcert the reader with analysis of motive or with irrelevant comment. (Grabo 116–17)

Early versification texts give less time to invention, but they do discuss conditions favorable to reflection (like listening to music), places for writing, and questions that might help the writer discover that first line.

The first college play writing texts also deal with the essentials of form, but they do not provide as many classifications or exercises, perhaps because play writing was usually taught in the most advanced undergraduate or graduate courses. George Pierce Baker, a Harvard professor, wrote one of the most popular of these texts. In *Dramatic Technique* (1919), he argues that play writing should be taught only to graduate students, and he speaks with dismay of the "recent mushroom growth" of such classes for undergraduates (v). Instead of dividing drama into types or formats, he discusses the essentials of all good drama—mental and physical action, character development, and dialogue. Separate chapters present methods of turning a subject into a plot, of achieving clarity and proportion, and of creating characters and dialogue, with examples provided from Greek, European, and British drama. Another frequently reprinted text was Scottish critic and playwright William Archer's *Play-Making: A Manual of Craftsmanship* from 1912, which devotes several chapters to each step of play writing: choosing a theme, characters, and a writing routine and then crafting the first act's exposition and foreshadowing, the second act's tension and suspension, and the third act's climax, anticlimax, and close. Archer provides many examples, primarily from Shakespeare and Ibsen, "the most generally accessible of playwrights" (prefatory note, np).

Although all of these books present sequences of assignments and advice intended to train writers, they recognize the doubts behind their mission, the attitude that the writer must be "born" and cannot be "made." In the foreword to his 1914 text, Robert Neal tries to specify that which cannot be taught:

> A last word—to those who scoff at "attempts to manufacture writers." This book is written to guide and help persons who wish to write short stories. But it is not written with the belief that short story writing, or any other form of literary composition, can be taught. It cannot. Literature is art, and art is not communicable. Theories of its methods and success can be inferred and explained; its

practical technique can frequently be explained and acquired. But neither theory nor technique makes art; the
living spirit is not in them. (xi)

Other textbook authors also recognize the need for a gift or inspiration while staunchly defending the value of instruction in
technique and critical reading:

This little treatise does not aim to create poets—Heaven
must do that; but it does seek to furnish those who have
poetic inspirations with the knowledge of how to master
the forms of expression. Poetry is first a gift, then an art—
both the gift and the art demand civilization. (Esenwein
and Roberts ix)

To open his text, George Pierce Baker argues for a writing curriculum by comparing creative writing to the other arts: "'The
dramatist is born, not made.' This common saying grants the
dramatist at least one experience of other artists, namely, birth,
but seeks to deny him the instruction in art granted the archi-
tect, the painter, the sculptor, and the musician" (*Dramatic
Technique* iii). These writers had reason to be defensive about
their new undertaking; their justifications were addressed to
colleagues who viewed their efforts as futile or anti-intellectual
as well as students who did not expect rigorous instruction in a
creative writing course.

Although detractors might have thought otherwise, most of
the first courses in all three genres consisted of a challenging
combination of workshop and lecture meetings. In lecture sessions once or twice a week, the teacher discussed required
readings, often from a literature anthology, and specific writing techniques and formats. In workshops—before the age of
ditto and xerox machines—students brought their manuscripts
to class and either the teacher or writer read the work aloud.
Then the teacher made an extended comment, perhaps drawing from the readings to illustrate a point, and students also
offered their opinions. In his text, William Carruth suggests
for workshops to convene during a single period of at least two
hours, instead of separate periods of one hour, to allow time
for reading and discussing the students' poetic exercises for

that day or revisions of their work from the day before as well as professional samples. He recommends an informal class structure:

> A classroom with straight rows of seats does not afford in any case the most congenial conditions for the enjoyment of poetry. It is especially unfavorable to verse writing and mutual criticism. If possible a verse-writing course should meet out-of-doors, or at least in a private study and around a table. Stiffness and conventionality must be dispelled. So far as may be, the class should be like a club of friends gathered for common enjoyment and helpful suggestion and criticism. In such surroundings it is easier to draw out the real thought and the serious consideration of even the shy members. (54)

Carruth recognized that this setup might attract "persons of light weight disposed to take the course as a joke" or "egotists inclined to use it as a personal forum" (54–55). He warns that the teacher must not tolerate such types, but instead should give the course seats to serious students—he suggests a class size of 12—who had taken freshman composition.

A famous course following this arrangement was George Pierce Baker's English 47, which enrolled primarily graduate students. Baker had written papers on acting when he studied with Wendell as a sophomore at Harvard; after Baker returned there as a teacher, Wendell advised him that scholarship on the drama would advance his career more quickly than work on argumentation and composition (Kinne 45). Baker's intention became to teach play writing and build an American theater tradition while also researching theater history. He began teaching English 14, a survey of early English drama, as well as meeting with students in his home to discuss modern plays and writing techniques, participating in drama clubs, and giving community talks on modern drama. Then he started a year-long seminar on play writing, English 46, at Radcliffe in 1903 and a similar course, English 47, at Harvard in 1905; in 1915 he began second-year courses for the best writers at both schools. Students had to submit a one-act play to gain permission to enter the beginning classes. Once enrolled, they wrote at least four plays following formats that Baker assigned: an adaptation of an assigned short story in one act, an adaptation of a story chosen by the student, an original one-act, and a play of at least three acts (Gelb and Gelb 270). Baker would also accept any other manuscripts that students wanted to submit to class review. Each week as the students sat around a large oak table, Baker read their work aloud and the group discussed it; in private conferences, he gave writers his own detailed responses to their work; in lecture and discussion sessions, he compared the play to the novel and short story, analyzed required readings, and pointed out techniques that the students might employ. In April of 1904, for example, he gave lectures to the Radcliffe class on low and high comedy, referring to George Meredith's "Essay on Comedy," Aristotle's *Poetics,* literary histories, various plays, and the students' own work (Kinne 94–100). In later years, he relied less on lectures, instead devoting more time to workshop sessions.

In 1914 at age 26, Eugene O'Neill came to Harvard to take the play writing course after he had spent one year at Dartmouth as a freshman and written *Bound East for Cardiff* and other plays. His application letter to Baker indicates the course's considerable reputation: "With my present training I might hope to become a mediocre journey-man playwright. It is just because I do not wish to be one, because I want to be an artist or nothing, that I am writing to you" (Kinne 193). While taking the course, O'Neill criticized Baker for teaching a too commercial and conventional form of drama, and he often acted superior to the other students, pushing his chair away from the table and grunting rudely in reaction to their plays. O'Neill accepted Baker's invitation to join the new advanced class, but he didn't return the next year.

In later years, O'Neill seems to have reappraised his teacher: he began to correspond with Baker frequently, sought his help with theater managers, and accepted an honorary degree Baker secured for him at Yale. When O'Neill wrote to Baker in 1919, he explained his long silence:

> I realize I must have seemed woefully lacking in gratitude
> because, seemingly, I have never had the decency to write—

and I know the interest you take in the work of your former students. But I'm really not as bad as that. In all honesty, I have waited more out of small-boy ambition than anything else. I was confident that the night would come when I could approach you with that digesting-canary grin, and, pointing to the fiery writing on the wall of some New York theatre, chortle triumphantly: "Look, Teacher! See what I done!" (Kinne 206)

When Baker died in 1935, O'Neill composed a letter for the *New York Times* concerning the important effects of Baker's belief in his students and his attention to technique:

Only those of us who had the privilege in the drama class of George Pierce Baker back in the dark age when the American theatre was still, for playwrights, the closed shop, star system, amusement racket, can know what a profound influence Professor Baker, who died last Sunday, exerted toward the encouragement and birth of modern American drama. . . .

In the face of this blank wall, the biggest need of the young playwright was for intelligent encouragement, to be helped to believe in the dawn of a new era in our theatre where he would have a chance, at least, to be heard. And of the rare few who had the unselfish faith and vision and love of the theatre to devote their life to this encouragement, Professor Baker's work stands pre-eminent. It is this encouragement which I—and I am sure all the playwrights who knew and studied under him—will always remember with the deepest appreciation.

Not that the technical points, the analysis of the practice of playmaking taught in his class, were not of inestimable value to us in learning our trade. But the most vital thing for us, as possible future artists and creators, to learn at that time (Good God! For anyone to learn anywhere at any time!) was to believe in our work and keep on believing. And to hope. He helped us to hope—and for that we owe him all the finest we have in memory of gratitude and friendship. (i)

Other students recorded their impressions of Baker's class. Like O'Neill, John Mason Brown, who entered Harvard in 1919 and later became an influential drama critic and a playwriting teacher at the Bread Loaf Writers' Conference, commented on Baker's devotion to the art and craft of drama:

> This Professor Baker who dared to teach such an unteachable subject as playwrighting was the least dogmatic of men. He had no Golden Rules of Dramaturgy. He did not pretend to be able to turn out playwrights in ten easy lessons. Indeed he did not claim to be able to turn them out at all. He was among the first to admit that dramatists are born, not made. But he did hope to be able to shorten the playwright's period of apprenticeship by granting him the same instruction in the essentials of his craft that the architect, the painter, the sculptor and the musician enjoyed in theirs. (540)

Heywood Broun, a class member who became a columnist and critic, wrote that English 47 provided technical instruction and an audience for the few with talent, but it also made better readers and thinkers of the rest. And, he noted, English 47 performed another important service by discouraging those budding playwrights who could profit from being discouraged. Thus Baker helped create "excellent young men who have gone straight from his classroom to Wall Street, and the ministry, and automobile accessories with all the nascent enthusiasm of a man just liberated from a great delusion." Broun also provides a humorous picture of the young writers' dramatic excesses:

> When I was in English 47, I remember that all our plays dealt with Life. None of us thought much of it at that. Few respected it and certainly no one was in favor of it. . . . Some of the playwrights in English 47 said that Life was a terrific tragedy. In their plays the hero shot himself, or the heroine, or both, as the circumstances might warrant, in the last act. The opposing school held that Life was a joke, a grim jest to be sure, cosmic rather than comic, but still mirthful. The plays by these authors ended with somebody ordering "Another small bottle of Pommerey" and laughing mockingly like a world-wise cynic. Bolshevism had not

been invented at this time, but Capital was severely handled, all the same. All our villains were recruited from the upper classes. Yet capitalism had an easy time of it compared to marriage. I do not remember that a single play I heard all year in 47, whether from Harvard or Radcliffe, had a single word of toleration, let alone praise, for marriage. (63)

Thomas Wolfe, whom Baker admitted in 1920 because Wolfe had been a member of the University of North Carolina Playmakers, found many of the plays "unreal, sterile, imitative, and derivative" (170). In *Of Time and the River,* he illustrates this judgment by describing the sentimental plots chosen by two students. A "wealthy young dawdler from Philadelphia" set his play in a French café:

Here one was introduced to all the gay, quaint, charming Frenchmen—to Papa Duval, the jolly proprietor, and Mama Duval, his rotund and no less jolly spouse, as well as to all the quaint and curious habitués that are so prolific in theatrical establishments of this order. One met, as well, that fixture of these places: old Monsieur Vernet, the crusty, crotchety, but kindly old gentleman who is the cafe's oldest customer and has had the same table in the corner by the window for more than thirty years. One saw again the familiar development of the comic situation—the day when Monsieur Vernet enters at his appointed time and finds at his table a total stranger, sacrilege! Imprecations! Tears, prayers, and entreaties on the part of Papa Duval and his wife, together with the stubborn refusal of the imperious stranger to move! (170–71)

A "sour and withered ex-reporter," old Seth Flint, chose dramatic coincidences and sentimental endings:

He wrote plays in which the babies got mixed up in the maternity ward of a great hospital, in which the rich man's child goes to the family of the little grocer, and the grocer's child grows up as the heir to an enormous fortune, with all the luxuries and securities of wealth around him. And he brought about the final resolution of this tangled scheme, the meeting of these scrambled children and their bewildered parents, with a skill of complication, a design of plot, a dexterity that was astonishing. (172)

Wolfe also describes Seth as an asset in class: he might write sentimentally, but he could unleash a "barbed but cleansing vulgarity" when the group discussed unrealistic dialogue like the following:

Irene (slowly with scorn and contempt in her voice). So—it has come to this! This is all your love amounts to—a little petty selfish thing! I had thought you were bigger than that, John.

John (desperately). But—but, my God, Irene—what am I to think? I found you in bed with him—my best friend! *(with difficulty)*. You know—that looks suspicious, to say the least!

Irene (softly—with amused contempt in her voice). You poor little man! And to think I thought your love was *so big*.

John (wildly). But I do love you, Irene. That's just the point.

Irene (with passionate scorn). Love! You don't know what love means! Love is bigger than that! Love is big enough for all things, all people. *(She extends her arms in an all-embracing gesture.)* My love takes in the world—it embraces all mankind! It is glamorous, wild, free as the wind, John.

John (slowly). Then you have had other lovers?

Irene: Lovers come, lovers go. *(She makes an impatient gesture.)* What is that? Nothing! Only love endures—my love which is greater than all.

Eugene [Thomas Wolfe] would writhe in his seat, and clench his hands convulsively. Then he would turn almost prayerfully to the bitter, mummified face of old Seth Flint for that barbed but cleansing vulgarity that always followed such a scene:

"Well?" Professor Hatcher [George Pierce Baker] would say, putting down the manuscript he had been reading, taking off his eye-glasses (which were attached to a ribbon of black silk) and looking around with a quizzical smile, an impassive expression on his fine, distinguished face. "Well?" he would say again urbanely, as no one answered. "Is there any comment?"

"What is she?" Seth would break the nervous silence with his rasping snarl. "Another of these society whores? You know," he continued, "you can find plenty of her kind for three dollars a throw without any of that fancy palaver."

Some of the class smiled faintly, painfully, and glanced at each other with slight shrugs of horror; others were grateful, felt pleasure well in them and said under their breath exultantly:

"Good old Seth! Good old Seth!"

"Her love is big enough for all things, is it?" said Seth. "I know a truck driver out in Denver I'll match against her any day."

Eugene and Ed Horton, a large and robust aspirant from the Iowa cornlands, roared with happy laughter, poking each other sharply in the ribs.

"Do you think the play will act?" some one said. "It seems to me that it comes pretty close to closet drama."

"If you ask me," said Seth, "it comes pretty close to water-closet drama. . . . No," he said sourly. "What the boy needs is a little experience. He ought to go out and get him a woman and get all this stuff off his mind. After that, he might sit down and write a play."

For a moment there was a very awkward silence, and Professor Hatcher smiled a trifle palely. Then, taking off his eyeglasses with a distinguished movement, he looked around and said:

"Is there any other comment?" (174–75)

Participation in the class could lead to having a play performed on Radcliffe's campus by the 47 Workshop, started by Baker in 1913. This small group of students, faculty, and townspeople usually gave four performances each year, of one-act and full-length plays by members of the class and other playwrights. Baker's students attended rehearsals and worked on lighting, scenery, and costumes to expand their knowledge of the theater. Authors were involved in every stage of production, with the goal being to create the best possible version of their intentions. Then each member of the audience, an invited group of 400 theater experts, submitted a written response to the author to guide further revisions. It was Harvard's unwillingness to provide any more support for this experimental theater than a small room for rehearsals and a lecture hall for performances that caused Baker to move his classes and theater to Yale in 1924 (Baker, two articles entitled "The 47 Workshop"). Heywood Broun reported the decision: "The score is Yale: 47; Harvard: 0" (Gelb and Gelb 604).

The creative writing class model of lecture and workshop left room for many variations, as in the first poetry writing courses at the University of Iowa. In 1897, Verse-Making Class had the following catalogue description: "Practice in metrical composition in the fixed forms of verse such as the heroic couplet, Spenserian stanza, ode, rondeau, sonnet, ballad, and song. Analysis of the best examples of these forms in English poetry. Informal discussions of artistic questions" (University of Iowa, Catalogue 1895–96 38). The instructor, George Cram ("Jig") Cook, had started college at Iowa and then spent his senior year at Harvard in 1893 before studying in Europe. At Harvard, he took English 12 with Barrett Wendell, describing in his diary the frustrations caused by that staunch critic:

> October 6, '92: I am discouraged to-day. I have done no good work since I have been here and the college year has been under way four days. I seem unable to write anything good in English 12. If I cannot write, why throw my life away in fruitless effort? My literary taste is not good. It is merely chance whether I like a thing which Barrett Wendell says is good. I am nineteen years old to-morrow, and for all I can see I am not doing as good work as I was doing a year ago. I will shut my teeth and go on patiently. I *will* succeed.

In the journal, he also bemoaned making a fool of himself in Charles Eliot Norton's Fine Arts 3: "Talked wildly and incoherently about 'theories of composition.' The Lord only knows what I meant to say" (Glaspell 48–49).

Cook returned to Iowa City with a desire to introduce students to the culture of the ancient world and modern Europe. He was quickly known as a wild one with a "hearty instinct against authority." His class met in loosely structured workshop and discussion sessions, as his wife Susan Glaspell later described: "He never reported an absence. If his students were interested they would come. If they weren't interested, why should they come? He would really rather they didn't. But they did come, wanting to see what charming truancy their teacher would next devise and gravely lead them to." He arranged for further critiquing sessions outside of class time at his room, which he shared with another teacher: "You sat by an open fire, and were given rum in your tea when you came to see them. There were Chinese hangings. Iowa City was not quite sure." Cook especially wanted to serve as a catalyst for those few who thought creatively, who could see beyond Iowa: he "talked to the dozen who knew what he was talking about, and let the others make what they could of it" (Glaspell 82–86). When war was declared against Spain in 1898, he left to join the Iowa Volunteer Infantry, and then went to Mexico to gather material for a novel, did truck farming in Iowa, and wrote for the *Chicago Evening Post* before starting the Provincetown Players with Susan Glaspell (Wilbers 36).

Another poetry writing teacher at Iowa was Edwin Ford Piper, a former participant in writing workshops that his chair, Clarke Ansley, had led at the University of Nebraska. His collections of poetry—*Barbed Wire* (1917), *Barbed Wire and Wayfarers* (1924), and *Paintrock Road* (1927)—reveal his commitment to regional themes. An avid collector of ballads and broadsides about the midwest and west, he was known as the "singing professor":

He virtually sang many of his poems; reading "Zebra Dun," he was a cowboy talking to his horse. When he said "whoa," it was not as a professor reading to class members for their souls' edification, but as a top-hand who cajoled his pinto or mustang.

When parts of a poem called for song—the lines shouted by a caller at a square dance—Professor Piper sang the lines

with all the enthusiasm and gusto of the old-time caller, in
time to the fiddles and "the big-bass viol." (Wallace 1)

Besides conducting these "singings," Piper discussed regional
authors in class and urged students to emulate them. At times,
his regionalist fervor may have hindered the students' development, as student Ruth V. Bortin has noted:

> Piper himself was always very tactful and supportive, but he
> had strong ideas of what he liked. I was writing a long poem
> about my Grandmother, which I saw as a psychological
> study (not that I knew any psychology then) but he wanted
> me to make a tale of pioneer life in Iowa. (Wilbers 11)

To encourage the better students, Piper participated in student literary clubs and conducted a special advanced class, with
voluntary attendance, in his basement office, which his student
and later colleague, John Frederick, described in an essay about
Piper:

> I am a member of another class—an informal one this
> time: Attendance is optional, but there are few of us who
> fail to find our way in the late afternoon to Mr. Piper's
> basement office, where we sit in nooks between bookcases
> or even share a table with heaps of papers and magazines,
> and read the stories and poems and essays we have written
> for the comments of one another and of our leader. In that
> group, as rarely elsewhere in my experience, there was
> practiced by Mr. Piper the principle of criticism which I
> believe to be the only right one for dealing with student
> work: "Something to praise, something to blame." (83)

Like those on drama and poetry writing, the first short story
courses followed the flexible model of lecture sessions and
workshops. These classes also offered students the opportunity
to read contemporary American and British fiction, then
taught in few literature classes. In the Art of the Short Story,
beginning in 1895 at the University of Chicago, Edwin H.
Lewis had students read Poe, Irving, and Hawthorne as well as
George Washington Cable, Joel Chandler Harris, Bret Harte,
William Dean Howells, Brander Matthews, Arthur Conan

Doyle, Octave Thanet, and Mary E. Wilkins (Barrett 41–44). In Newcomb College's course The Short Story, introduced in 1908 when the few literature classes taught at Newcomb concerned English literature before 1900, students read Poe, Hawthorne, Bret Harte, George Cable, Lafcadio Hearn, and Edith Wharton. At Iowa, the first course in short story writing, instituted in 1900, was by its second year offered in a two-semester sequence, with one term devoted to study of "typical stories by Poe, Hawthorne, and their successors" and one to successful writing practice taught through workshop sessions and lectures on readings and technique (University of Iowa, Catalogue 1901–02 112).

Opposition to the Campus

In 1915, these innovative classes were infrequent: they had not yet become a key form of training for writers. This decade was instead a period of rebellion against academia, against teachers holding onto an American canon of Whittier, Bryant, Longfellow, and Holmes and offering a genteel and narrow vision of life that seemed irrelevant in the violent decade of the first world war and its aftermath. Barrett Wendell became a straw man for some, a representative of the older Boston Brahmin tradition. Van Wyck Brooks felt that his "tender-minded" teacher "stood for the seekers of lost trails" and that he "cherished his Harvard memories of a world that was gone" (425–26).

Many young writers turned to each other, and away from their teachers, for their mentoring. At Princeton, F. Scott Fitzgerald shared his writing and reading with John Peale Bishop and Edmund Wilson, sophomores when he entered as a freshman in 1913 (LeVot 38–39). In a letter to his son in 1940, Fitzgerald described the contrast he found between these fellow students and his English teachers:

You need, at the beginning, some enthusiast who also knows his way around—John Peale Bishop performed that office for me at Princeton. I had always dabbled in verse but he made me see, in the course of a couple of months, the difference between poetry and non-poetry. After that one of my first discoveries was that some of the professors who were teaching poetry really hated it and didn't know what it was about. I got in a series of endless scraps with them so that finally I dropped English altogether. (Turnbull 88)

In New York, recent college graduates like Edward Arlington Robinson, John Bishop, Edmund Wilson, Marianne Moore, and Edna St. Vincent Millay congregated before and after the war, extending their college groups by reading each other's work and discussing new poetry they found on the shelves of the Washington Square Book Shop. They wrote for little magazines such as *Poetry* (1912) and *Others* (1915), which provided an outlet for experimental poems by Pound, Stevens, Eliot, Sandburg, Moore, Edgar Lee Masters, and Kenneth Burke (Munson 33–36). Some also began to work for publishing houses. Armed with a letter of introduction from Barrett Wendell, Max Perkins was hired by Scribner's in 1910. Over the objections of older editors, he signed Fitzgerald's *This Side of Paradise* in 1919. The Washington Square Players and the Provincetown Players, many of whom were former students of George Pierce Baker, began performing experimental drama in 1915. In Provincetown, the wharf theater provided a backdrop of real waves through the open back doors for the first staging of O'Neill's *Bound East for Cardiff,* a play that George Pierce Baker had criticized in English 47. George Cram Cook organized this theater because the Washington Square Players seemed too 3 traditional to him: they had rejected one of his plays as being too radical. This tradition of rebellion continued in Europe, involving Dos Passos, Hemingway, e. e. cummings, Dashiell Hammett, Edmund Wilson, and others: military service provided, as Malcolm Cowley described it, "college-extension courses for a generation of writers," as did the postwar artistic circles in Paris (*Exile's Return* 38).

Escape from academia and lessons from real writers were sought not only in Greenwich Village and Montparnasse: a seedy, quasi-glamorous start could also be found at the newspaper. Although beginners made only ten dollars a week in 1915, a writer could learn about factual narrative and detailed observation there, a training that influenced the form of the modern novel. Frost, Sandburg, Dreiser, Mencken, Stephen Crane, Sinclair Lewis, and Hemingway held jobs as cub reporters. At the *Kansas City Star* in 1917, Hemingway served under "big, curly-haired, broken-nosed Lionel Moise, a brilliant reporter who was also a poet, a cop-slugger, a heartbreaker, a singer of barroom ballads, and a great teller of barroom stories" (Cowley, *The Literary Situation* 162–63, footnote 1).

Another "rebellion" tradition of creative writing also developed in Nashville, Iowa City, and other rural university sites before the war, where teachers and students reacted against a restrictive university curriculum by meeting in literary and debate clubs. Writers' clubs formed in Iowa City around 1890 to provide a place where students and faculty could read their own work and receive criticism. George Cram Cook took part in the founding of one club while he was still a student. Clarke Fisher Ansley, chair of the English department from 1899 to 1917, joined four writers' clubs. In 1921, professors John Frederick and Frank Luther Mott organized the Saturday Luncheon Club, to extend the education of young writers by bringing in outside speakers. With very little money, they secured Robert Frost, Carl Sandburg, Sherwood Anderson, and Clarence Darrow as guests. Mott's Times Club and SPCS (Society for Prevention of Cruelty to Speakers) also brought in prominent writers, but their most anxiously awaited speaker was one who never arrived, Gertrude Stein, whose plane was grounded in Waukesha, Wisconsin, during a snowstorm.

A writers' group began in Nashville in 1903, the year John Crowe Ransom entered Vanderbilt as a freshman. Early discussions at the apartment of Sidney Hirsch, a poet and linguist not associated with the university, often focused on philosophy, as sophomore William Elliott, later a political scientist and poet, described in a letter concerning a 1915 session:

> Right now I am having what the debutantes twitter "a gorgeous time." Nat Hirsch, Stanley Johnson, Donald Davidson, John Ransom, and Sidney Hirsch were the company last night and it was Olympian. I am living in rare altitudes

this summer, though I haven't gone to Monteagle yet. We get together often and I can feel myself grow. . . .

Out on the Hirsches' porch, with the cigar ends glowing occasionally, a debate always insured from the nature of the company, it is *The* Happiness. Last night it was the Unity of Being that was under discussion, Johnny maintaining a dualism at least—*Elan Vital* and Material Expression, I, admitting a logical duality, maintaining a pluralistic Individuality of Being, but a Metaphysical unity. I learned a great deal. (Cowan 4)

By the fall of 1916, Ransom, by then an instructor, was encouraging these friends to discuss *vers libre* and other forms of "new poetry" and was sharing his first verse writing attempts with them (Cowan 21). Most of the participants returned from the war by 1919, with a stronger interest in writing. In 1921, they asked senior Allen Tate to join them. The group began publishing *The Fugitive* in 1922 with poems by Ransom, Davidson, Tate, and other members—with financial support not from the university but from subscriptions and donations. By that time they had formed an exacting writers' workshop, as Donald Davidson described their meetings:

First, we gave strict attention, from the beginning, to the *form* of poetry. The very nature of our meetings facilitated and intensified such attention, and probably influenced Fugitive habits of composition. Every poem was read aloud by the poet himself, while the members of the group had before them typed copies of the poem. The reading aloud might be followed by a murmur of compliments, but often enough there was a period of ruminative silence before anyone said a word. Then discussion began, and it was likely to be ruthless in its exposure of any technical weakness as to rhyme, meter, imagery, metaphor and was often minute in analysis of details. Praise for good performance was rarely lacking, though some excellent poems might find the group sharply divided in judgment. But even the best poems might exhibit some imperfection in the first draft. It was understood that our examination would be skeptical. A poem had to prove its strength, if possible its perfection, in all its parts. The better the poem, the greater the need for a perfect finish. Any inequality in technical performance was sure to be detected. It was not enough for a poem to be impressive in a general way. Poems that were merely pleasant, or conventional, or mediocre did not attract much comment. (21)

Bringing the Off-Campus to the Campus

In the 1920s, more of this off-campus tradition began to take place on campus, as writers returned home from abroad and from Greenwich Village, often in search of a secure living, and as universities became more receptive to new courses and to modern literature. For better *and* worse, college creative writing instruction, from that decade onward, has been shaped not only by prewar course models, but also by the back-porch and salon writing group experiences of many American writers before 1920.

This shift to the university class as the site of mentoring and apprenticeships involved the many established authors who took jobs as composition instructors with full teaching duties or as writers-in-residence with limited responsibilities after 1920. Miami University of Ohio made playwright Percy MacKaye, who had studied with George Pierce Baker at Harvard, a writer-in-residence in 1920, building him a much-publicized studio and requiring him to perform few academic duties (Thompson and Winnick 263). Robert Frost was a professor of English at Amherst for parts of 1917 to 1920, and then went to the University of Michigan during 1921–22 as a poet-in-residence with no instructional responsibilities. Thomas Wolfe served, in a much less glamorous capacity, as a composition instructor at New York University from 1922 to 1930. T. S. Eliot was a professor of poetry at Harvard during the 1932–33 school year.

Authors brought with them a focus on the students' own independent projects, and thus they put less emphasis on required readings, lectures, and assignment sequences: they were creating on-campus versions of critique sessions like those the Fugitives had held in Nashville. In 1921, in a proposal for a new summer course for writers in Middlebury, Vermont, Robert Frost stated that the students would never be assigned exercises of any type: the teacher would no more consider making assignments to students than they would think of making assignments to him. Richard Wilbur, who was educated at Amherst and Harvard and taught at Wellesley, has also expressed this common attitude: "I don't want to turn my students into clever executors of formal problems. I want them to start the way any kind of poet starts, with the matter, with the urge, and then find out what aids—what formal aids—might make the urge clearest" (Garrett 43). Michael Denis Browne, like many other teachers, has asserted that this freer teaching style reflects the identity of modern poetry:

> I think that to encourage vivid, wide associational thinking is just as much a discipline as going through forms. I personally don't approve of either going through forms or using rhymes. I think that they're not useful any more, because I think that we can say that repetition and pushing apart the gaps between objects and their actions, reassigning the functions metaphorically, is what poetry is tending to do now. *(Teaching Creative Writing* 44)

Many creative writing teachers—like Ransom, Davidson, Wallace Stegner, and Theodore Roethke—continued the tradition of extensive critical reading in the creative writing course. But the focus was changing from treating students as readers and writers working within a long tradition to treating them as writers creating themselves.

As "professional" teachers and methods entered the university and the commitment to creative writing was thus extended, the numbers and types of workshop courses began to increase. John Crowe Ransom taught the first creative writing course at Vanderbilt, English 9, when he returned from Europe in 1919 (Cowan 20, note 30). Harry T. Baker, who published a text on fiction writing in 1916 when he taught at Illinois, established an undergraduate course in the short story and one in creative writing of all types at Goucher College in the 1920s. He wrote that teachers should avoid rule-bound instruction so that they could encourage, and possibly inspire, those students with talent. In the 1920s, Wisconsin instituted a year's course in play writing, with "an acceptable scenario" required for admission (University of Wisconsin, Catalogue 1920–21 153). The University of Missouri had a course in "technique of English verse, with practice in metrical composition" (University of Missouri, Catalogue 1920–21 161). Before 1930, Penn State's English department had begun offering a short story workshop and an array of professional theater courses for undergraduates:

Eng. Lit. 90. Playwriting (3).—Elementary principles of dramatic composition, combined with the dramatization of short stories. Recitation 3 hours; 1st semester.

Eng. Lit. 91. Dramatic Technique (3).—Various forms of drama studied in detail. Native materials, as subjects for drama, will be examined, and the methods by which they may be used will be investigated. Recitation 3 hours; 2nd semester.

Eng. Lit. 92. Dramatic Production (3).—Acting and directing for students who are planning to teach English. Students will act in and direct several series of one-act plays. Consent of instructor required. Recitation 3 hours; 1st semester.

Eng. Lit. 93. Stagecraft (3).—The technical problems connected with play producing in the professional and non-professional theatre. Practical work in the designing and construction of scenery, make-up, costume-design, and lighting. Recitation 3 hours; 2nd semester. (Pennsylvania State College, Catalogue 1928–29 242)

By 1930, around 45 percent of American colleges had at least one creative writing course, with many of them offering two or three on different genres.

To extend the class experience and continue small group traditions, professors also began to incorporate more extracurricular writing activities into the English department. At Iowa, John Frederick involved students in *Midland,* a regional literary journal. Frank Luther Mott, who came to campus in 1921, acted as advisor to the *Iowa Literary Magazine.* In the summer of 1939, Edwin Piper invited 11 writers, including Donald Davidson, to attend his graduate writing seminar, offer readings, and participate in small group meetings. In workshop sessions, students and their leader reacted to work that had been mimeographed and made available to them before the meeting—very much as the Fugitive group had in Nashville. Particular attention was afforded to the best students in these first sessions of the Iowa Writers' Workshop:

> Each year 25 or 30 students are admitted to the Workshop. Instruction is tailor-made to the individual. At first, the student holds weekly conferences with Prof. Wilbur Schramm, director of the Workshop. These conferences may last thirty minutes or several hours, according to the problems presented. Poets soon consult Paul Engle, playwrights Prof. Leigh Sowers, some of the prose writers Prof. Frank L. Mott. As the students develop they are organized into small groups that meet weekly or bi-weekly. The more expert a student becomes, the less need he has of frequent conferences and meetings, and the more time he needs for his own writing. The most envied group in the Workshop is the "top ten" who meet fortnightly at the homes of Schramm and Engle. (Wilbers 53)

By 1940, this structure provided the model for other writers' workshops and conferences that might last several days or weeks and might offer undergraduate or graduate credit. The Bread Loaf Writers' Conference began at Middlebury College in 1926, and others followed at Hollins, Kenyon, and Wesleyan. After World War II, growth accelerated—more conferences and workshops, undergraduate and graduate degree programs, visiting professors, and writers-in-residence.

These developments have made creative writing instruction more professional, with real mentors, writing groups, and writing projects, but they have also caused problems for both students and teachers. Students looking for general improvement in their writing or reading may feel lost in some classes. Professional writers may feel separated from the rest of the English department. They may neglect students or their own writing, as George Garrett of the University of Virginia has stated:

It is a balancing act, because teaching in itself is an art form, too, and it is very satisfactory. There's a danger not only that you'll spend too much time on your own writing at the expense of the students (which I find myself doing, and then I have to take a step back), there's also the other danger on the other side. You get so engaged with the teaching that you are no longer a practitioner, and at that point you're in trouble, too, because you're not communicating the professional's approach to this. (*Teaching Creative Writing* 89–90)

In the introduction to his anthology on teaching creative writing, Joseph Moxley describes the lack of adequate reading, intellectual rigor, and grounding in technique that may attend the college workshop centered on student writing. The writing group, a model developed by well-read and self-directed adults, may not always be appropriate for inexperienced students. In the Moxley anthology, Eve Shelnutt points to lack of critical reading training and to an anti-intellectualism possible in creative writing programs, especially in M.F.A. and B.F.A. degrees that may require few literature courses.

Today professional writers teach at the university, but wonder whether they should be there—as do many of their colleagues in English departments—and even assert that writing can't be taught. Growth has not brought certainty concerning their mission or methods, as we hear in this 1966 declaration from a famous writing teacher, Wallace Stegner, himself an alumnus of the Iowa Writers' Workshop:

We have never pretended that we taught young writers much of anything—in fact, we have drawn back from the danger of being *too* influential—but it has been our faith that we helped create an environment in which they could learn and grow. It would be interesting to know whether or not we succeeded in providing such an environment, or whether they would have been better off keeping a diary in the Peace Corps, or working in a steel mill, or writing for a newspaper. Were these writers, I wonder, warmed and brightened by any promethean fire they found at Stanford, or did they merely strain their eyes trying to learn? (x)

Whatever the doubts of writers and teachers, creative writing programs have continued to grow. In 1970, 817 schools offered at least one creative writing course, employing 543 full-time and 1,245 part-time faculty to teach these courses. In 1981, 26 percent of nonintroductory writing courses offered in English departments concerned creative writing (Witte 27). While accountants, librarians, engineers, and physical therapists created curricula for their specialties, creative writing programs were also developing, with similar involvement from practitioners and academics. But growth has not solved all problems. The "unteachableness" of writing, of creativity, of genius lies at the root of continuing self-deprecation and doubt. The forging of a separate identity and separate degree programs has led to separation, from other composition teachers within and outside of English departments as well as from the literature faculty. Creative writing teachers are often branded as being too detached or self-centered, as being uninterested in really teaching writing. So their doubts and successes have been their own, without much input from a larger writing community. Their students have missed other writing courses as they moved through the sequences offered in the creative genres. And students in journalism, technical writing, and other genres have missed the experience with language, dialogue, description, and plot construction that can be gained in a creative writing class.

6

Education for Journalism

Journalism may now seem like a completely separate discipline from creative writing, but its history is very similar. In this discipline, also, instruction began in late nineteenth-century English departments, as part of the drive toward specialization in education. Like their colleagues in creative writing, journalism instructors adopted practical methodologies—involving professional writing formats and workshop sessions—to distinguish these new courses from purely academic subjects, especially from freshman composition, and to emulate professional practice. The next step was to bring in experienced writers as teachers. These developments brought praise and blame: excitement over new, practical learning along with the cry of anti-intellectualism.

Journalism Instruction Comes to Campus

The first formal college journalism instruction concerned printing skills. Along with programs in law, engineering, and business, Robert E. Lee instituted college instruction in newspaper printing at Washington College (later Washington and Lee) to create industrial growth in the south and to fit young southern gentry for leadership roles. In 1869, students apprenticed at

Lafferty and Company Printers in Lexington; John J. Lafferty was soon appointed as "superintendent of instruction in Typography and Stenography" (Nash 8). Kansas State College of Agriculture and Applied Science began teaching printing in 1873. Cornell, Denver University, and the University of Missouri also hired local printers to offer this practical training.

By 1890, the growth of the newspaper business had shown that specialized training would be needed for other parts of the trade. The number of newspapers almost doubled from 1870 to 1880, a decade when population increased only 30 percent. There were 12,000 American newspapers by 1890 (Mott, *American Journalism* 411). These papers across the country covered politics, social events, religion, business, and everything else in news articles, human interest stories, and editorials. The newspaper's increasing size as well as its emphasis on local research and individual interpretations gave reporters greater influence. The excesses of the "penny press," sensationalized accounts of politics and society, also gave a greater field to critics. Thus journalism was viewed as a growing if troubled profession for which a new specialized preparation might be needed.

Not everyone agreed, however, that young writers should be trained through college courses. Many self-made journalists looked on college graduates as proud and hard to instruct: real journalists, they asserted, learned their trade in the street and at the newspaper office. Horace Greeley, influential owner and editor of the *New York Tribune,* supposedly roared out while banging his desk: "Of all horned cattle, deliver me from a college graduate." In an 1875 interview, Horace White, formerly of the *Chicago Tribune,* made the same point more politely: "I think that journalists must train themselves by practice in the several departments of the profession" (Wingate 15–16, 77–81). *Philadelphia Times* editor Eugene M. Camp summarized this widespread distrust of college preparation for journalism in an address entitled "Journalists, Born or Made," delivered at the University of Pennsylvania in 1888:

Indeed, they [the "older class of journalists"] do not stop by saying that the colleges cannot give instruction that will be advantageous to future journalists, but they go so far as to attack the college men themselves and to taunt them with impractibility [*sic*]. They point out that college graduates who enter newspaper offices are generally distanced by the upstarts who can do little more than spell. (7)

Other newspaper editors, agreeing with the widespread criticism of an effete education, thought that colleges could provide a valuable starting place if they began to offer the practical training that had previously occurred only in the newspaper office. They wanted students to spend their final two years, or perhaps their only two years, taking vocational journalism courses. A 1930 American Association of Newspaper Editors' report summarized this long-held attitude: "Such editors frankly want the departments of journalism to be trade schools. They want to be relieved of the torturous work of teaching copyreading, office routine, and the elements of news gathering" ("Report of the Committee on Schools of Journalism" 144).

Another group of editors and writers valued the college's liberal arts training, especially in history, political science, economics, and languages, and argued that college graduates—even the proud ones—had more to offer than high school students. But they did not necessarily want to make room in this curriculum for practical journalism courses:

We believe that the boy entering newspaper life needs, prior to coming into the shop, more than all else a background of systematic study in the arts and sciences as extensive as his time, money and capabilities will permit. We think it is more important a hundred fold than that he should know how to write a good hand, how to read type in the forms, how to put together in orderly sequence the "add bulletins," "sub night leads," "eliminate trivial," "kill unimportant," and "add day leads" which go to make up an Associated Press report. Shop practice, as often has been said on this floor, can be acquired in a year, even amid the rush and turmoil of the newspaper office. Systematic study of societal relations, of history, economics, the basic sciences, languages and a keen appreciation for cultural values is difficult at the close of a ten-hour day of reportorial leg work, a day which frequently must be stretched until only time for hasty meals and such sleep as is absolutely essential is secured. ("Report of the Committee on Schools of Journalism" 143–44)

Though the opposition was thus to continue, a small number of journalists and academicians spoke of the value of combining traditional liberal arts study with journalism classes in a four- or five-year college program. This model found early support from Joseph Pulitzer, publisher of the *New York World;* Whitelaw Reid, editor of the *New York Tribune;* Charles Eliot Norton, president of Harvard; and Andrew White, president of Cornell. Reid and others frequently compared journalism to law, medicine, and engineering, recognizing that those professions were instituting rigorous college training and that journalism needed a similar academic structure to increase its quality and status. The busy modern newspaper office, like the law firm and doctor's office, they maintained, was no longer the place to train apprentices. Reid's frequently quoted speech, "Journalism as a Career and Educational Preparation for It," presented in 1872 at New York University and then published in *Scribner's,* emphasized this comparison: "It is of their [newspaper editors'] possible training in a School of Journalism, to be appended to the regular college course, as one of the additional features of university instruction, like the School of Mines, or Medicine, or Law, that I speak" (204). Charles Emory Smith of *The Philadelphia Press* argued in 1888 that journalists needed training even more than those other professionals:

The principles of law are clearly defined, well established and laid down in the books where the student may find them. The principles and rules of journalism are nowhere presented in any such precise way and are not accessible in the same form. Though less definitely determined they are susceptible of clear statement and illustration. There are no practical text-books, though there are special studies which may be recommended and pursued by way of preparation. In fact, the rules of journalism are what the best-trained and most skillful master of the art make, and they can best be imparted by those who constitute the authorities. (Camp 9)

Joseph Pulitzer's 1904 will, in which he endowed a journalism school at Columbia, also focused on the advantages that specialized training gave to other professions and could give to journalism:

> There are now special schools for instruction for lawyers, physicians, clergymen, military and naval officers, engineers, architects, and artists, but none for the instruction of journalists. That all other professionals and not journalism should have the advantage of special training seems to me contrary to reason. ("The Columbia Agreement" 14)

Like creative writing, journalism came to the university at a time when readership and interest in the genre had increased, when various types of professional training were being discussed, and when at least some practitioners felt that training might occur at the college, where other types of specialized programs were prospering. Land-grant universities, like Missouri, Wisconsin, and Nebraska, looking for practical commitments and an increased role for their liberal arts departments, began teaching journalism around 1900. Other state and private schools instituted courses and programs as the debate concerning this new instruction continued.

The First Classes, Teachers, and Texts

Before 1910, at least one news writing class was being offered at Missouri, Pennsylvania, Chicago, Wisconsin, Temple, Iowa, Iowa State, Indiana, Michigan, Nebraska, Oregon, North Dakota, Bessie Tift College for women in Georgia, and other schools. At that time, no academicians had been specifically trained to teach journalism: because it was being approached as "writing," English professors usually took on the job. Edwin M. Hopkins, who taught the first journalism course at Kansas in 1894, had undergraduate and doctoral degrees in English from Princeton; his publications concerned *Piers Plowman* and composition instruction. He later became director of a new Department of Journalism, head of the English department, and president of NCTE. John William Cunliffe, professor of English at Wisconsin from 1907 to 1912, associate director of the

School of Journalism at Columbia from 1912 to 1920 and director from 1920 to 1923, had graduate degrees in classics and modern languages from the University of London; he published literature anthologies and histories of English and French literature. These men did not have newspaper experience, nor did they conduct research on journalism.

To staff the new classes, universities also sought out experienced reporters or editors with an academic background, at least a college degree, and perhaps some teaching experience: such rare breeds were often charged with planning new courses and departments. Joseph French Johnson was graduated from Harvard in 1878, studied political economy in Germany, worked for the *Springfield Republican* and *The Chicago Tribune,* and founded *The Spokane Spokesman* before he accepted the position as professor in charge of journalism in the Wharton School of Business at the University of Pennsylvania in 1893. James Melvin Lee, a B.A. from Wesleyan University in Connecticut, had taught English at a seminary for one year and had been on the staff of eight newspapers and magazines before he joined New York University as a lecturer in journalism in 1910 and became director of the journalism department in 1911. Talcot Williams had a B.A. and M.A. from Amherst, had been a staffer for the *New York World* and *New York Sun,* but had no teaching experience when he became director of Columbia's School of Journalism in 1912. Walter Williams, first president of the American Association of Schools and Departments of Journalism, had a high school degree, training in printing, and editorial experience at five newspapers when he became dean of the new School of Journalism and professor of history and principles of journalism at the University of Missouri in 1908.

These teachers had few textbooks to rely on. Journalists wrote the first instructional manuals in an anecdotal, entertaining form for an audience of young people—not necessarily college students—interested in learning about the career. *Haney's Guide to Authorship* from 1867 gives general advice: "In setting about literary work the mind should be freed as much as possible from annoyance, and the health good. . . . An excess of epithet is a besetting sin with young authors. . . . Above all things stop when you have done" (13–15). Julian Ralph's *The*

Making of a Journalist from 1903 offers chatty anecdotes from his career—on following hunches, racing other reporters, and making trains. The most crucial ability, he maintains, cannot be taught: reporters must be born with that "news sense," a "nose for news," a "sixth sense," a mysterious "instinct" that causes them to go to the right place and ask the right questions.

Between 1900 and 1920, newspaper editors and college teachers produced more practical texts on reporting. Since news writing was often the sole journalism offering, these books introduce the field generally before turning to reporting itself. The preface to *Practical Journalism* (1903) by Edwin L. Shuman, editor of the *Chicago Record-Herald,* states that the book will explain "how the work of the best and largest daily papers is done" from a "plain and matter-of-fact" viewpoint (vii–viii). It starts with a history of the press and then deals with different newspaper jobs, the Sunday supplement, newspaper art, advertising, country papers, and libel and copyright law as well as writing and editing. *Making a Newspaper* (1907) by John L. Given, who had been a reporter at the New York *Evening Sun,* starts with a history of American journalism and then offers practical advice about printing, advertising, circulation, ads, libel law, and copyright law before turning to news and feature writing.

Like their creative writing counterparts, these books reveal the tentativeness of advanced writing instruction, the continuing debate over its validity, over whether writers are "born" or can be "made." Many of them recognize the requirement of genius as they also call for better education:

> Editorial writing is both a craft and an art. As a craft it may be taught and learned, like printing or bookkeeping. As an art only its elementary principles can be acquired. The art of it must be born largely with the individual. This volume deals in the main with editorial writing as a craft. Its purpose is to instruct the apprentice in the elements of the work—to acquaint him with the tools he must use in his prospective vocation. Beyond this point the genius of the individual writer must make for success or failure or mediocrity. (Spencer, *Editorial Writing* 16)

If the profession would accept this "making" of writers, these books assert, modern journalism could avoid nineteenth-century penny press excesses: in correcting these wrongs lay a strong justification for college journalism programs. These authors argue that college-trained journalists could change the profession's negative image by reporting facts objectively and by shaping stories to illustrate moral beliefs. In *Types of News Writing* (1916), Willard Bleyer of the University of Wisconsin defines the news as "anything timely that interests a number of readers" (6), but he criticizes the writing and selling of "sensational, ghastly, and scandalous phases of the news" as similar to "the selling of habit-forming drugs and adulterated food, acts now forbidden by law" (9). He asserts that the reporter must aim for a "wholesome effect," a "constructive purpose"; a story about a suicide or crime, for example, should not create a criminal hero but should emphasize protection against wrongdoing. *News Writing*, written in 1917 by Matthew Lyle Spencer of Lawrence College, defines the news as "any accurate fact or idea that will interest a large number of readers": its qualities are "strangeness, abnormality, unexpectedness, nearness of the events" (26). He recognizes the American love of abnormalities and extremes, listing these stories as being of exceptional interest: "a burglar stealing a Bible or returning a baby's mite box, a calf with two heads, a dog committing suicide, a husband divorcing his wife so that she may marry a man whom she loves better" (30). He argues, however, that this preference indicates a desire for instruction that the journalist can exploit: "It is not, therefore, that American men and women are interested in the sins and misfortunes of others that they read stories of crime and unhallowed love, but that such stories present new problems, new life situations, or new phases of old problems and old situations" (28). In many early texts, these corrective definitions of the news take up as much space as the anecdotal information on writing it.

As journalism programs developed after 1910, with separate courses on history, ethics, advertising, and business management as well as reporting and editing, new types of writing textbooks appeared. They contain very little material on journalism history or the newspaper business, leaving those subjects to other textbooks and classes. They rely on a simple definition of the news as "anything timely that interests a number of people" without alluding to the sensationalized stories of earlier generations and without suggesting that news writers shape their facts around moralistic themes. As journalism standards improved, journalism courses no longer needed a moral imperative to defend their existence.

Since these texts give less attention to all of journalism, they can concentrate on writing. Often the advice focuses self-consciously on the disparity between the news article and the freshman theme:

> Put the point of your whole story into the first sentence, and the shorter the sentence the better. Whether the story be two columns or two inches long, cram the marrow of it into the first paragraph. Banish the school-essay idea that there must be an introduction or preliminary explanation of any kind. . . . Every newspaper report should answer the questions, "What? Who? Where? When? Why?" and should do it in the first paragraph as nearly as possible. (Shuman 59–60)

Spencer's *Editorial Writing*, published in 1924, also includes derisive comments concerning the forms of discourse: "It is appreciated that the four forms of writing were studied at distressing length during high-school and early college years, and probably forgotten promptly or only hazily remembered" (110). This book gives short examples of the four forms of discourse but then notes that purely narrative and descriptive editorials are "all but non-existent" (102) and that exposition and argumentation are not distinct categories since both styles of writing can serve as persuasion. At the beginning of *Types of News Writing*, Bleyer states that news stories can be narration, description, exposition, or a combination of them, but he doesn't mention these categories again.

In their attempt to "banish the school-essay," textbook writers began to focus on formats of news writing. Bleyer divides the news into common story types: those covering fires and accidents, crime, criminal and civil courts, weather, sports, and society. Spencer's *News Writing* deals with effective leads and story structure before turning to court, accident, crime, sports, and society reporting. Like many other journalism books, this text only briefly mentions paragraphs as the smaller units within these story structures—with a new indention being used to create emphasis or a transition. Like their creative writing counterparts, these texts dissociate themselves from school writing by accentuating the format requirements of the specific genre and by deemphasizing current/traditional divisions of discourse. The variations within the genre, types of news stories being like types of poetry, could create a term's or a year's syllabus.

Many of these books contain sophisticated sections on audience analysis—generally ignored in freshman texts from that period. Spencer's *Editorial Writing* talks about the superficiality of American readers:

> Readers in the mass are not philosophers or deep students of any school of political thought. They are a practical working host, concerned with only the most pressing realities of life, craving to be amused, to be made to laugh or cry over passing occurrences, but not to be made to think too hard over any subject that does not concern them vitally. (68)

According to Spencer, editorialists must carefully examine the desires of these readers: "the underlying motive that inspires everybody to read is self-interest." Thus a subject must be presented "in such a way that readers would see its application to themselves and their own affairs" (61–62). Spencer also understood that editorials would not, and should not, always reach the entire newspaper audience, that they should at times take on complex matters, such as international relations, to influence a "thoughtful minority": "It is well for the editorial writer to remember that the confidence of a single strong leader in an editorial or an editorial page often is worth more than the commendation of hundreds of individuals within the ranks of semi-ignorance" (69). Spencer also wanted his students to consider how the reader scans a page:

> The average reader opens his paper at the editorial page as he does any other page, holding the paper tiringly high, his

left hand grasping one page, his right hand the other. His eye slips from the masthead, not to the first editorial below, but to the first headline at the right. If the heading is not attractive, he passes on to the first one that is, where he reads a sentence or so, his eye again passing on if his attention is not instantly arrested. (100)

To illustrate formats and writing techniques, these books present many examples from published news articles, usually with introductory sentences explaining the features being illustrated: "the following is a typical football story," "the restraint and dignity of tone of the stories are worth close study," "note the suspensive effect of the following leads" (Spencer, *News Writing* 171, 200, 230). For such pieces, Spencer's *News Writing* draws from the *Atlanta Constitution, Chicago Herald, Chicago Tribune, Kansas City Star, Los Angeles Times, New York Times,* and other papers. In his preface, Spencer points to this use of contemporary writing as another feature distinguishing journalism texts from those for freshman composition.

While these texts present professional products and descriptions of their features, their exercises also draw students into the process of creating finished copy. In the 1924 second edition of *Essentials in Journalism,* originally published in 1912, Harry Harrington, director of the Medill School of Journalism at Northwestern University, and Theodore Frankenberg, a reporter, reproduce a transcript of a phone interview between a reporter and a store manager concerning a robbery. They next provide the resulting article so that students can examine the interpretation and arrangement of the data (67–69). In other exercises, students are given lists of facts and instructed to eliminate the unimportant or unsubstantiated details, elaborate on the others, and write a lively story. This text also provides revision tasks, requiring students to correct stilted diction, ineffective leads, and wordy stories. In Spencer's *News Writing,* the exercises concern careful research and analysis, outlining, writing, and editing, as the following directions indicate:

Most of the following stories held front-page positions on leading metropolitan dailies. Explain their story values. (285)

Put the following details in proper sequence for a suicide story. (290)

Correct such of the following leads as need correction. Where the age of the person, his place of residence, or similar details necessary to an effective lead are lacking, supply them. (291)

In 1921, Grant Milnor Hyde of the University of Wisconsin supplemented the texts then available on news and editorial writing by preparing the first separate *Handbook for Newspaper Workers,* for use by students and new reporters, with sections on grammar, punctuation, diction, style, accuracy, and typographic styles as well as headline writing, copyreading, proofreading, and the handling of pictures and cuts. Hyde says in the preface that his intentions are practical, that he wants students to move beyond the stilted tone of their school work to the active voice of professional writing. He may have intended this text, in part, as a rebuttal to the other famous handbook from Wisconsin, Edwin Woolley's *Handbook of Composition* from 1907, used in freshman composition classes throughout the country.

In his book for freshmen, Woolley relies on a developed grammatical vocabulary, giving directions like "a predicate substantive completing a finite verb should be in the nominative case" (35). Usage is stipulated by definite rules. Under split infinitive, for example, the student is told, "Do not put an adverb or phrase between an infinitive and its sign *to*" (77). Hyde also relies on grammar terminology, but he provides explanations of these terms. After the introduction to present participles, for example, the reader finds in parentheses "the verb form ending in *ing*" (10). Hyde also gives reasons for correct usages, by referring to their effect on readers: Woolley states that "*there is* should be followed by a singular noun; *there are,* by a plural noun or nouns" (30); Hyde states that "*there* as a sentence beginning is to be avoided because it lacks emphasis and wastes space" (20). Even when the two authors make the same point, Hyde does so in a simpler, more practical tone: Woolley has, "for the sake of beginning the sentence with words that deserve distinction, it is often advantageous to place *however, therefore, nevertheless, moreover, also* and the like, within the sentences they introduce rather than at the beginning" (76); Hyde advises, "*However, nevertheless, moreover,* etc., are weak introductions to sentences; place them inside" (20). Woolley cautions students to avoid the improprieties found in newspapers: "Newspaper usage does not establish an expression as good English. The best newspapers set high standards, and oblige their writers to study 'style books' similar to this Handbook, in order to avoid offenses against good English. But many newspapers have no such standards, and employ provincial and vulgar language" (2). He also warns against "hackneyed newspaper mannerisms" that have "arisen through the effort of writers to adorn their style where no ornament was needed, or to introduce a forced humor, or to avoid repetition of the same word" (16–17). Hyde defends the modern newspaper and notes the exaggerations of its detractors: "Critics of American newspapers are wont to speak of newspaper writing with a sneer and to brand it with the terms, 'journalese' or 'newspaper English,' while they point to incorrect usage, bad diction, and careless English in the press" (66).

Many of the journalism courses before 1910 were distinguished from freshman composition by the inclusion of lectures on journalism history and newspaper organization, material appearing in the first texts. Teachers also brought their own research interests and views on journalism to the new courses. In the late 1870s, University of Missouri students used interviewing methods and wrote news pieces in political economy courses taught by David Russell McAnally of the English department, whose father had been a newspaper editor and whose own research concerned social customs, particularly relating to courtship and marriage. In his first news writing courses, beginning in 1884, McAnally emphasized "vigorous and clear English" and journalism's role in social research. The class also involved news writing assignments, work on literary styles, and discussion of English essayists. In 1894, at the University of Kansas, Edwin M. Hopkins, head of the English department, offered a "highly experimental" course on newspaper writing to three students, to investigate social forces and the power of the press in shaping modern thought (O'Dell 35–36, 49).

These first courses introduced news writing, but not the daily activities of the journalist. Courses taught after 1910, like the later textbooks, moved further away from freshman composition by emphasizing the writing process and formats of contemporary journalism, and thus provided the beginnings of a more specialized type of career education. Teachers assigned story types from the textbooks, like accident, crime, and society articles, requiring students to use the facts or first drafts given in exercises. In classroom meetings, students learned principles of journalism writing, such as the five "W's," critiqued each other's exercises, and studied professional samples. As a supplement to the textbook, teachers began looking for opportunities to teach students more about "real" news gathering and writing.

Before these classes began, practical journalism work had been taking place on campus through school newspapers, usually begun as weeklies that published literary pieces. One of the first was the *Dartmouth Gazette* (1799–1820), which had Daniel Webster among its student writers (Mott, *American Journalism* 206). Students at Georgetown started the *College Minerva* during the 1820s, writing copies out in longhand (Daley 215). At Tulane, fraternity members instituted *The Rat* and the *Gazette* in 1890 as single typewritten sheets tacked to bulletin boards (Dyer 157). Although some colleges, like the University of Chicago, instituted and supported school newspapers, they were more frequently run by students who secured funding from advertising and faced stern administrative and faculty protests over negative stories (Goodspeed 252). After the administration closed down an early Vanderbilt paper because of its criticisms of the library and faculty, the new *Hustler* was allowed to begin printing in 1890 only after its staff agreed to the following stipulation: "If in the judgment of the faculty the paper is conducted in a manner to injure the University, they may dispose the editor-in-chief" (Mims 121).

Harvard had several papers before 1850 that closed either because of lack of funding or faculty protest. The biweekly *Magenta,* later the *Crimson,* changing names as the school color changed, began in 1873. The student writers and editors were fairly free of faculty control: they operated out of university quarters, but they secured their own advertising and subscribers and monitored their own finances. The first issue had paragraph-length articles concerning poor library policies, inadequate sidewalks, and the need for better lighting in the reading room as well as praise for renovations to the campus chapel. Subsequent papers dealt with campus and town issues, teachers (one being labeled as "a little tin god on wheels"), and sports. Issues were published alternately by Riverside Press and John Wilson and Sons in Cambridge and later by an on-campus press office. In 1882 the *Crimson* became a weekly; in 1883 it merged with a competitor and became a daily. An 1899 article recorded an ordinary, hectic workday of the students who served as the board of directors, managing editor, editors, reporters, and proofreaders:

> At an hour in the morning depending on the time at which he got to bed the previous evening, and also on his lectures, the managing editor comes to the office and begins his day's work. After a glance at his memorandum books, he is ready to make out the list of assignments.
>
> This is the foundation of the forthcoming issue, but while laying it he is never free from interruptions. Editors come in to find out whether they are to have work given them or not, and they sit around talking and laughing and poking fun at the managing editor while he tries to write, and they wait. Often other officers of the board appear with something to discuss. More than one person calls with the various purposes of pointing out that an organization in which he is interested has not been given enough prominence as of late. . . . A freshman is easy to dispose of. But if the caller is an instructor or a graduate, the task of pacifying him, or explaining the situation or, occasionally, making him see he is asking for the impossible, may be both hard and unavoidable. A familiar classmate who rides his hobbyhorse into the office is likely to be attacked bodily, and dumped into a huge waste-paper basket near the telephone box, provided enough editors are present. The most exciting of all the morning interruptions can be caused by an angry business manager, who comes waving a printer's bill for extra work.

Before lunch time the assignment list is made out and hung up, and the office can lapse into quiet until evening. Those who come to it in the afternoon come to write and to be left alone.

By half-past seven the lights are lit and the copy box begins its merciless accompaniment to the printer's sharp cry, "Carp-e-e." This box is primarily an invention for conveying manuscript from the desk to the printing room. From then on the managing editor's business is to keep his head, and to see that order and reason prevails in all matters concerning the paper and himself. Candidates come in with botched "stories" and wonderful excuses. All have to be attended to and set on the straight path promptly. Editors must needs be coaxed into getting down to their work, and then persuaded to keep at it until they are finished. Newspaper correspondents arrive and put the unvarying question: "Is there anything tonight?" and then leave for the time being, or else go to their side room to work according to the answer given by the managing editor. . . . More interesting but less common are interruptions caused by the president of the board when he has some editorial question which he cannot settle alone. Indeed, so many and so various are the things which occur on a busy evening that one might say that the time which the managing editor can rescue from interruptions is none too much for the work of editing copy for the printers.

Little by little, as the hours wear on, the hurry and worry lessen, and the office becomes quieter and emptier, until only the proofreader remains for company. Finally the managing editor has nothing to do but to sit back in his chair and keep awake until he has been called up by the Associated Press, and the printers have told him that the paper is full and all is well. (Lawless 22–24)

A more controlled classroom version of such a newsroom, many professors thought, could become a vital component of a practical journalism class. In 1904, when Edwin M. Hopkins of the University of Kansas introduced his second news writing course, his students wrote articles for campus publication: "In the fall of 1904 a volunteer section of freshman rhetoric was organized into a group of reporters, and the newspaper class proper into a corps of editors; beats were assigned, and edited. Matter was sent to the local papers including the *University Daily Kansan"* (O'Dell 49). When the Missouri School of Journalism opened in 1908, the faculty began sponsoring a four-page daily, *The University Missourian,* a city newspaper that provided a laboratory for the students who covered news and features of interest to the community, edited copy, secured advertising, and circulated the paper in town. Each day, their classes combined lectures with production sessions:

> The bell in the tower of Switzler Hall rings for eight o'clock classes; the day's work begins. In one room a professor lectures on the writing of editorials . . . in the news room a group of students gather for work on the University Missourian. The work is divided into hours according to the general University program. At nine o'clock come other lectures—advertising in one room, the history and principles of journalism in another—and other student reporters assemble for assignments. . . . After ten o'clock virtually all the work of the School is of practical nature, the formal lectures having been given in the first two hours. Pencils scratch busily, typewriters click, the telephone rings. This is the "laboratory" of the School of Journalism. (S. Williams 29–30)

Starting in 1893, in the University of Pennsylvania's Wharton School of Business, Joseph French Johnson offered a course in newspaper practice, in which "students were given various assignments to report university functions, ball games, etc." Although the class didn't produce a daily, it used the college and Philadelphia, according to the course description, as a "news laboratory" (Lee 10).

More and More Practical

By 1925, only 17 states did not have journalism programs. Fifty universities offered an undergraduate major; thirty-five of them provided instruction on the graduate level; eight also had a specialization in teaching journalism. Fourteen universities housed their programs within separate schools of journalism; 34 had journalism departments; and two had journalism majors or emphases within English departments. Many other universities had one or two journalism writing courses or advanced composition courses with journalism components, usually within their English departments. Of the 10,000 college graduates then working as journalists, over 50 percent had graduated from journalism programs ("Journalism Education in the United States"). By that time, most schools or departments offered courses on the history of journalism, comparative journalism, public opinion, and ethics of the press as well as news writing, editorial writing, feature story writing, book reviewing, and music and drama criticism. Some also offered magazine writing, advertising and business management, layout design, cartooning, and journalism education (Flint 84–85).

Dichotomies between the approach of English teachers like Woolley and new journalism specialists like Hyde had not boded well for the development of a journalism curriculum in English departments. Teachers with newspaper experience usually had academic training and publications that did not match the established expectations for promotion. The new lab courses seemed anti-intellectual to many English professors. The additional courses in journalism history, business practice, and advertising fit even less well with departmental goals. The American Association of Teachers in Journalism, begun in 1912, propelled the movement to separate quarters. Along with the American Association of Schools and Departments in Journalism, formed in 1917, this organization declared that all journalism courses should provide professional training and should be taught by journalism specialists, and thus should not be a variety of advanced composition offered by English professors: "nonjournalistic teaching of journalism will no more be tolerated by public opinion than non-engineering teaching of engineering or non-medical teaching of medicine or non-architectural teaching of architecture." The association even suggested, but never passed, a resolution requiring all journalism professors hired after 1929 to have five years' experience at a newspaper (Will, "Concerning the Status of Teachers" 18).

In classes taught after 1920, the instruction became ever more practical, with less reliance on exercises, fewer assignment sequences, and less general instruction on writing. Grant Hyde found this change a critical one:

Most of us have progressed beyond the classroom "make-believe" exercises of early days. Our student reportorial exercises are actual newspaper stories written for print; our copy desk groups handle copy hot off the wire; our classes in editorial writing are sanctum conferences; our feature articles appear in the Sunday supplements." ("Raising the Quality of Students" 19–20)

To provide students with more thorough practical training than could be gained from a campus weekly or daily, professors secured new partnerships with local papers. In 1924, 40 University of Oregon student reporters wrote feature stories for the *Sunday Morning Register* in Eugene. In Baton Rouge, students at Louisiana State University had a separate newsroom at the local paper:

A news room, 17 by 28 feet, for the exclusive use of the instructors and of the class in Reporting and Newspaper Practice in the Louisiana State University Department of Journalism was included in the plans of the recently constructed and strictly modern building of the Baton Rouge "States-Times," an evening daily. This room is now furnished and equipped for journalism instruction. Facilities are provided for giving students practical training in news gathering and writing, copy-reading, headline writing, rewriting, proof-reading, and make-up. Students receive assignments from the city editor, who is a member of the journalism faculty, make regular news runs, and gather a large part of the local news used by the paper. Associated Press and syndicate copy are also handled by the students.

All the work of students in this class is done under actual newspaper conditions and surroundings. They write stories, read copy, and build headlines with the sound of the linotype machines, telegraph instruments, and telephone bells in their ears. They learn how to work under pressure

and to observe the "deadline". After the advanced students have a few months of such experience they are put in
full charge for a day of the editorial department of the
"State-Times". The classes have done some of their best
work on these occasions, and these "journalism editions"
have received editorial commendation from some of the
leading dailies of the State.

In the late spring, the advanced classes in journalism
spend a day in New Orleans where they visit the plants of
"The Times-Picayune," "The New Orleans Item," and
"The New Orleans States." ("Notes of the Schools" 34)

By 1927, the University of Iowa's reporting courses also had
an extensive practical component that involved several local
newspapers:

They publish a newspaper six days every week, not merely
a campus paper, but a newspaper, with a city page, or
pages, and a large Associated Press telegraph report. They
issue five other student publications, all of which are
printed in their own shop. Once a year they travel 120
miles in order to do all of the work on five editions of the
Des Moines Register, the largest newspaper in the state.
Twice a year they go to another town to issue two other
daily newspapers. Once a year the class in community
weekly goes to a nearby town, gathers and writes all the
news and editorials, designs, writes and sells all the advertising for a 24-page community weekly. Members of the
various classes serve as reporters and copyreaders for the
evening newspaper published in Iowa City. The class in
editorial writing in addition to writing the editorials for
the Daily Iowan, their own paper, are now writing editorials for the Press-Citizen, the evening newspaper. One
member of the class is sponsor for the high school newspaper. (Lazell 29)

At Iowa and other schools, this laboratory model also shaped
the newer classes in editorial writing, the feature story, magazine writing, and music and drama criticism.

Reactions

All of this quick movement toward practical education was not without its critics. By 1925 most journalists felt that new reporters needed a college education and some professional training. But many felt that the growing number of practical courses was leading students too far away from the liberal arts. In 1936, when Burges Johnson of Syracuse University surveyed managing editors of newspapers in cities having more than a 100,000 population, he found that only eight of 67 respondents approved of schools of journalism and two of these editors thought that the instruction should occur only at the graduate level. Many respondents made claims such as, "Men coming from most journalism schools have not sufficiently broad knowledge or broad cultural background for our purposes," and thus they preferred to hire liberal arts graduates, with a "well-founded general education." These editors also questioned the journalism school's formalistic approach to news stories:

> Today we don't see the newspaper as merely a mechanical device for collecting the news and putting it out in a 6 "W" form. We feel that the news is but the springboard and that it is the handling of this news by a professional type of mind, bringing in background, significance, future possibilities—all as an integrated whole—which promises most for American journalism.

Because of the attention to formats and to frenetic daily press work, these editors contended, journalism graduates lacked basic writing skills: "training in the use of clear, correct, written English is most important and evidently most neglected" (B. Johnson, *Classes in "Journalistic Writing"* 18–21).

In his 1938 doctoral dissertation, Vernon Nash contended that Johnson had written a "leading" letter when he sent his survey to these editors: the frequent hiring of journalism school graduates and the support given by state press associations to university programs revealed more widespread acceptance of journalism schools than Johnson's data would indicate. Nash interpreted the editors' responses as indicating dissatisfaction with the current curriculum instead of a complete rejection of journalism education (32). As journalism teachers and courses had divorced themselves from an English-department style of teaching writing, Nash asserted, they had gone too far: teachers coming from newspaper offices seemed to be just haphazardly teaching what occurred there. Thus, Nash declared, journalism courses were becoming unsubstantial, with students running here and there without learning basic thinking and writing skills and without doing enough reading. Just covering whatever happened on campus or in town for a term could not introduce students to the principles and practice of real city journalism, as Curtis B. MacDougall of Northwestern University also noted in *The Journalism Quarterly* in 1938:

> Both of these so-called "laboratory" methods, however, fall short because the student usually goes through the year handling nothing but speeches, meetings and interviews. Although it is valuable to have reporters proficient in covering Parent-Teacher meetings, there are many other types of assignment which the cub will receive early in his postgraduate career for which such training does not prepare him adequately. Fires, kidnapings, important accidents and similar events cannot be depended upon to occur conveniently as the proper chapters are being read by reporting students, and, if they should, cooperating city editors are not going to allow amateurs to handle the stories even though the student's program of class hours permits him the freedom to do so. (284)

Since the practical approach seemed to ignore the full job and influence of a reporter, teachers in the 1940s began to feel that discussion of law, ethics, and public opinion—of the reporter's role in society—should be added to the news writing course. The political events of that decade showed that students would need lectures on current news sources (correspondents, press associations, syndicates, beat and assignment reporters) and historical research. Regular class work might involve more reading of news articles and essays as well as more attention to the fundamentals of grammar and style. The creation of a two- or three-course sequence on news writing and of courses on editorial and feature writing provided some leeway for a combination of approaches, for practical and theoretical learning. To incorporate the new emphases, many programs decreased their lab component, curtailing involvement with local papers and re-instituting school newspapers as extracurricular activities.

Even with the uncertainties concerning curriculum, journalism programs continued to grow. In each decade, new journalism departments and colleges opened: by 1980, there were over 200 with courses in newspaper writing and editing, business and corporate journalism, magazine writing and editing, production, and business. At some schools, journalism became part of a department or college of mass communications that might also house—although not always cordially—newer courses in public relations, advertising, broadcast news, radio and television production, photojournalism, media law, media research, international media, and film. In 1960, 11,000 students were majoring in these fields; in 1973, 48,000; in 1984, over 78,000 (Cole 4; Peterson 3).

Like creative writing, journalism was first taught by English professors who had little experience with the genre itself, in courses that combined attention to grammar and style with exercises on formats and reading assignments. As the numbers of classes grew, the discipline's own professionals entered the university, bringing a more practical model of instruction, with less emphasis on basic writing skills and less general reading. These teachers sponsored journalism's departure from the English department, although some programs have remained there, primarily in smaller colleges. With the physical departure came professional separation, leading often to mistrust and competition, with English teachers thinking that journalism involves only sterile formats and with journalism teachers thinking that English means impractical belles-lettres.

This separation has allowed journalism classes and programs to prosper. But it has secluded journalism teachers from a larger discussion of writing and created unnecessary enmities. Like other writing instructors, journalism teachers continue to debate the validity of their own work, and especially the correct combination of theory and practice: of reading and writing, of basic writing skills and professional formats, of liberal arts education and career training. These teachers now prepare students not just for news reporting but also for the feature writing and technical editing central to newspaper, magazine, and trade journal production, genres with which other college teachers could provide assistance. That journalists work in another building and have colleagues in television production and media law should not keep them from communicating with other teachers who prepare students to be writers.

7

"Professional Writing" in Agriculture, Engineering, and Business

At the end of the nineteenth century, jobs were available, and success possible, in newspaper, magazine, and book publishing. Journalism training, and to a lesser extent creative writing instruction, could lead to employment. By this time, the growing business and engineering community also needed trained writers and editors. As degree curricula expanded, with fewer humanities requirements and more technical training, some change seemed necessary to insure literate employees. Business managers, engineers, and agricultural extension agents would not be able to rely on their high school and freshman training or on the shrinking number of college humanities requirements—or on secretaries and clerks—to meet their specialized communication needs.

The number of undergraduate students seeking technical instruction began growing steadily by the end of the nineteenth century. By 1900, 10 percent of college graduates majored in agriculture and forestry, engineering, and business; by 1950, one-third of all graduates majored in those fields. In 1905, six American colleges had business departments, with fewer than one percent of undergraduate males enrolled in them; by 1950 schools of business enrolled one out of four male undergraduates (Cheit 4, 27). By 1980, 24 percent of the total undergraduate population was majoring in business, 11 percent in engineering, and 2 percent in agriculture and forestry, for a total of 37 percent of college men and women (*Digest of Education Statistics* 198, 200).

Although these new programs consisted at first of a few courses tacked onto a liberal arts degree, students soon began spending more time studying their specific disciplines, as information concerning them increased and as each one made its bid for intellectual respectability and academic power. In 1909, the percentage of time occupied by the major varied from 7 percent to 34 percent, with most programs occupying between 14 and 25 percent of the four years (Veysey 36). In successive decades, and especially after World War II, the major began to involve more time—by the 1960s, generally 27–40 percent (*Missions of the College Curriculum* 187). The newer professional disciplines occupied the highest percentage, with business and agriculture at 50 or 60 percent and engineering often at 70 or 80. This movement toward specialization reduced the study of history, political science, literature, philosophy, and foreign language; it also meant that technical students did less writing in college. Most schools retained a one- or two-semester freshman writing requirement, combining modes of exposition with writing about literature. Students also took other freshman and sophomore classes involving papers and essay exams. But in the increasing number of—often large—classes concerning the theory and practice of a specific technical discipline, there might be few writing assignments.

That students therefore lacked a general education background and writing skills was often maintained, but with little effect. Although occasional strident criticisms, like the Society for the Promotion of Engineering Education's Hammond reports in the late 1940s, generated interest in basic requirements, the time given to academic specialties never significantly decreased. But the protest concerning student literacy had one result, in the creation of advanced courses in technical and business writing, offered through journalism and English departments. Like creative writing and reporting courses, these new technical and business writing classes obtained a distinct identity because of their focus on professional formats. But because they were not viewed as preparation for a distinct career and they were not staffed by specialists, these courses did not immediately engender writing programs or obtain the academic standing given to the new offerings in journalism and creative writing.

Agriculture, Engineering, and Business Enter the University

In early American education, instruction in the natural sciences might be part of a senior course in philosophy, often taught by the university president to connect the workings of nature to divine law (Veysey 2). By the early nineteenth century, almost every college had one or two science professors who could take over the senior course and provide lab demonstrations (Rudolph, *Curriculum* 104). In 1802 Yale appointed Benjamin Silliman as professor of chemistry, geology, and mineralogy. Columbia University created a chair in agricultural chemistry in the 1840s.

Vocational science programs did best at newer schools, where they did not conflict with an entrenched liberal arts curriculum. At West Point, established by Congress in 1802, students studied mathematics, chemistry, military engineering, drawing, and French (Rudolph, *Curriculum* 62). In 1819, the first private engineering institution was founded in Norwich, Vermont, by a former army commandant (Eddy 10); in 1823, the first agricultural school, the Gardner Lyceum, opened in Maine (Cheit 17). The Rensselaer Polytechnic Institute, which opened in Troy, New York, in 1824, had the mission of helping farmers to apply scientific knowledge to agriculture. Steven Van Rensselaer described his purpose in founding the college: "My principal object is to qualify teachers for instructing the sons and daughters of farmers and mechanics, by lectures or otherwise, in the application of experimental chemistry, philosophy, and natural history to agriculture, domestic economy, the arts, and manufactures" (Eddy 10). Besides supplying agricultural leaders, Rensselaer Polytechnic graduated engineers who helped design and build the new highways, bridges, canals, and railroads necessary for western development (Mann 4).

When vocational scientific education first entered older liberal arts schools, it was kept separate from the other programs. In 1846, Yale established two professorships—in agricultural and practical chemistry (Eddy 10). In 1859, the college opened a three-year school of applied chemistry with lower admissions standards and a separate budget: teachers rented lab space from the university and equipped it with their own funds; tuition and lab charges paid their salaries. A similarly structured School of Engineering was added in 1852, a chair of metallurgy in 1855, a professor of industrial mechanics and physics in 1859, and professors of agriculture, botany, and zoology in 1864 (Kirby 89–103).

By the Civil War, scientific information seemed crucial to increasing agricultural production and domestic manufacture. More secure programs in laboratory sciences, engineering, and agriculture came with congressional support for the land grant act of 1862. To receive funding, many state universities, like those in Georgia, Tennessee, Delaware, Missouri, Minnesota, Florida, and Louisiana, began vocational programs; separate agricultural and mechanical colleges were founded in Michigan, Kansas, Pennsylvania, Maryland, and Iowa (Eddy 49–50).

As these curricula were becoming well established, a few universities also introduced college business courses. Before the Civil War, even the largest American businesses were administered by small staffs of office workers, sometimes just the entrepreneur and a clerk. One of the oldest and most prosperous firms, E. I. du Pont de Nemours and Co., a gunpowder manufacturer in Wilmington, Delaware, was run by Henry du Pont from 1850 to 1889 out of an office by his mill. His largest staff of clerks consisted of four men and a boy. Du Pont wrote out his own letters, an average of 6,000 a year, with a quill pen. Larger organizations weren't formed until after the Civil War, to meet the growing need for products and services. The typewriter, first patented in 1868, moved slowly into the business world and created employment for women who took over the chore of writing letters. Schools of penmanship soon disappeared; customers began accepting letters with a signature as the only personal mark. After a patent for carbon paper was applied for in 1872, copies of letters could be kept and filed, and then the files themselves attained business status (Douglas 126, 131).

By 1910, high schools had begun to respond to the expanse of trade and manufacturing by instituting commercial programs combining instruction in typewriting and stenography with business math and accounting, advertising and salesmanship, and business English (Lyon 584). Large cities also had separate high schools of commerce where students prepared to be stenographers, typewriters, bookkeepers, and office clerks. Their English courses usually involved some literary study along with units on spelling, punctuation, and letter writing (Webster).

By 1910, the colleges had also begun offering business classes. The Illinois legislature voted in 1900 for a "course in preparation for business," to be supervised by David Kinley, professor of economics at the University of Illinois. In that year, New York University established its School of Commerce, Accounts, and Finance. By 1905, Wisconsin, Pennsylvania, Chicago, and Northwestern had also instituted programs in commerce that combined new offerings with liberal arts courses. At the University of Pennsylvania's Wharton School of Business in 1910, students took statistics, public law and politics, political administration, political history, public administration, municipal government, the United States constitution, and comparative constitution study as well as transportation methods, geography of commerce, business law and practice, accounting, banking, and finance. At the University of Chicago, students majoring in trade and industry took history and political science courses along with contracts, bills and notes, taxation, accounting, and the financial history of the United States.

As practical courses increased, many professionals and academics did not like what they had wrought. Around 1900, critics began a new opposition, stating that the technical movement had gone too far. With agriculture programs just beginning to gain support from professional organizations like the National Grange and with business programs just starting up, the major reaction to the students' inadequate training in liberal arts and writing came from engineers, as was discussed in chapter 2. Even with harsh criticism from industry leaders, however, few engineering schools redeveloped extensive general education: the emphasis remained on a core of engineering fundamentals and specialized technical training (Eddy 217). But they did make attempts to give the student better training in writing in a class or two, a more practical goal that seemed important to engineering faculty and easier to obtain. Ironically, concern for liberal arts training did not carry over to a "liberal arts" approach to writing. In his presidential address to the American Institute of Electrical Engineers in 1902, Charles P. Steinmetz spoke against teaching a "florid" literary or journalistic style:

> We hear that college graduates have no mastery of language, cannot express themselves logically, and it is therefore recommended that more time be devoted to literature and instruction in the English language. But as long as we do not teach logic, but have English taught by philologists, more or less of the character of the florid newspaper style, that is to write very many words on a very small subject, no useful results can be expected. (1148)

In 1903, Bancroft Gherardi of the same organization also criticized the current freshman curriculum of literary readings and analysis and offered his definition of the best practical approach to writing: "From this point of view discipline in English is not to be regarded as producing mere literary polish, but as enforcing correct thinking in regard to each and every question upon which [the student] has to write" (582). Another industry leader, J. G. White, had specific content in mind for a course that would enroll engineering students: "it may be necessary to have a considerable part of the training incorporated into the writing of laboratory reports, examination papers, and other similar documents" (576).

While this discussion was going on in engineering journals and at conferences, teachers of agriculture and business also began to examine the needs of their students, acting without as clear a mandate from their professional leaders. Although agricultural agents and researchers did not push for changes, some agriculture professors argued that additional writing training might be helpful—if it was practical. Harry R. O'Brien of the Oklahoma Agricultural and Mechanical College, for example, criticized older English department methodologies in his 1914 call for technical writing training:

> We have been going on in the same old rut, teaching farmers how to get culture, how to write glowing descriptions, how to get local color into narratives; when instead we should be setting these farmers to putting practical knowledge into clear, concise English. We should be teaching them how to describe the workings of an ensilage cutter or a milking machine, how to relate the life history of a grasshopper or a liverfluke. Many of the men who have come from the doors of our colleges have stepped out with almost no technical training in the art of writing on agricultural subjects. They give as the reason that much of the time spent in the composition class was time lost, as far as their practical writing was concerned. They learned to write in college when they wrote papers in their technical courses, or when they wrote articles for the student agricultural paper. If they did not learn it in this way, they learned by hard experience after they were out in the world. (471)

Professors involved with new business programs, such as Joseph French Johnson, who taught at the University of Pennsylvania and then at New York University, recognized that students who would be taking increasing numbers of courses in accounting, finance, and management would also need practical business writing training. David Kinley made business writing the only required course in Illinois's new program.

By 1910, many professionals and teachers were willing to accept the concept of practical writing instruction for advanced students, even if they were not willing to make room for more liberal arts courses. But because English and journalism programs both taught writing, with journalists perhaps seeming more like kindred professionals because of their practical outlook, two different types of technical and business writing training began to develop. In the period right after 1900, as late entrants into engineering and some agriculture programs and almost immediate entrants into college business curricula, courses from both departments gave definition to technical writing—the new "humanities" addition to the increasingly specialized college training.

Agricultural and Industrial Journalism

When journalism courses and professors arrived on campus after 1900 as the writing teachers who dealt with "real" writing, they seemed like a natural group to provide instruction to students in the new technical fields, to improve the letter, article, and report writing that so appalled industry leaders. Part of their mission and funding involved that immediate role, especially at land-grant colleges. By the 1920s, students in some agriculture and engineering programs took the regular news writing and editing classes to learn about press releases and articles, feature story writing, and other formats. At the University of Montana, for example, technical students took news writing classes to learn about addressing the public:

> They come from the school of forestry, business administration, library science, physical education, and to some extent from among those who are preparing for teaching. In the case of the forestry students the purpose for enrollment in journalism courses, usually reporting and editorial writing, is to provide a background for their forestry courses in public relations. With the others the prevailing motive appears to be a desire to learn how to sell their ideas to the public in the community which they expect to serve. Perhaps 10 percent of our enrollment in reporting courses comes from these sources. (Simmons 36)

At Minnesota, also, around 10 percent of the students in news and editing classes came from other professional disciplines. Not all journalism programs, however, welcomed such students. At Columbia and Northwestern, schools that had well-established curricula for training journalists, such enrollees were discouraged: "we attach great importance to having a homogeneous group of students who all intend to enter the profession" (Simmons 37).

Because of the problems created by mixed classes, professional schools often called on the journalism faculty to teach separate sections for science students. John O. Simmons recorded the request for a three-hour required course in agricultural journalism from the dean of the college of agriculture at Syracuse: "'I want you to give our students the essentials of writing for the news and agricultural press—with the emphasis on agriculture. Many of our graduates are taking positions in farm bureau and directional work for farmers. They must cooperate with the press to make their efforts bring results'" (Simmons 33). These separate classes formed a major part of the journalism curriculum at some technical institutions, as Stewart Robinson, professor of journalism at North Carolina State College of Agriculture and Engineering, noted in 1927:

> The work done in this institution so far . . . has been in the main in the nature of service work, that is helping our students who are taking courses leading to such vocations as county agents, vocational teachers of agriculture, textile employees, engineers, and so on, to understand the theory of news, learn how to locate, uncover, and write news and feature articles, learn to make contacts with newspaper executives, etc. (Drewry 36–37)

Articles in early issues of *The Journalism Quarterly* frequently refer to these classes as "nonprofessional" journalism, as in this definition that stipulates their secondary role in the students' career preparation:

> The "nonprofessional" teacher offers service courses to students in technical and professional colleges to enable them to get their occasional writings into form for publication. Service courses in this category are offered to boys who plan to become farm agents, to girls who plan to become home economics teachers or home advisers, to engineering students who look forward to writing special articles for engineering journals expressing their opinions or discussing the work of their companies. The students here involved have no interest in writing about anything but their own work. They may find later that they will edit a farm bureau paper to help them in farm advisory work, or they will publish a service bureau paper of some other type

as a side line; but they will then be practicing another profession and will give but a fraction of their time to the press. They will be content to do amateur work in journalism but they cannot afford to do amateur work in the line of their principal endeavor. They foresee this as students and are able to give but a fraction of their college time to journalism. They are not professional students building a specialty on top of general knowledge of the field as a whole; they are dabblers, trying to learn enough about the tricks of the trade to keep from making the grossest journalistic errors, and to have some sense of the ways in which the power of the press can be used to make their other regular work effective. (Murphy 49–50)

For these classes, usually with titles of agricultural or engineering journalism, teachers could rely on information concerning formats and style from a regular journalism text while requiring students to write on technical topics and read professional journals and bulletins. They could also choose one of the few textbooks written for specialized journalism classes. *Agricultural Journalism* by Nelson Antrim Crawford, director of information for the United States Department of Agriculture, and Charles Elkins Rogers, professor of industrial journalism at Kansas State Agricultural College, was first published in 1926 and reedited twice. The authors begin by talking about the audience for such a text. A half century earlier, they assert, farmers read Greeley's *New York Tribune* and perhaps one of the few agricultural journals and rarely wrote for publication. But since then, city dailies and country weeklies had begun employing agricultural writers, and the agricultural scientist, extension specialist, and farmer had begun to write for daily agricultural newspapers, farm magazines, and agricultural bulletins and newsletters. This book, then, would teach students to read printed material and respond to it effectively. Like journalism texts, it achieves those goals by providing instruction and examples concerning a series of formats: the agricultural news story, feature story, interpretive article, editorial, crop and market report, and women's column. It also contains advice on marketing agricultural copy and a short agricultural style sheet.

Although technical journalism courses never became universal, many schools offered them as electives after 1910. North Carolina State had courses in both agricultural journalism and industrial journalism. Alabama Polytechnic Institute had agricultural journalism and engineering journalism; the University of Florida offered a six-hour semester course in agricultural journalism (Drewry 37–39). Iowa State College, Illinois, and Wisconsin also instituted agricultural journalism as an advanced elective. In the 1930s, Drexel offered a course in technical journalism covering "articles on technical subjects associated with engineering, business, and economics; preparation of technical matter for the non-technical reader." Oklahoma A&M offered an elective in engineering journalism (Fountain 53, 59).

But as journalism schools grew in size and stature, they became less willing to devote resources to this general service role. In fact, the course labels themselves began to take on new meaning—as preparation for specialized journalists, not as a requirement or elective for engineering and agriculture majors. When New York University's Department of Journalism sponsored a Forum in Industrial Journalism in 1914 and 1915, its purpose was to "acquaint young men and women of the university world with the opportunities the business press offered for life work" (A. Wilson 5). The forum's speakers argued that specialized training should be made available to prepare journalism students, especially those with technical work experience, for jobs at the 800 trade and technical journals then being printed in the United States (Root 12). Speakers representing journals like *Dry Goods Economist, American Engineer,* and *Railway Age Gazette* sought dedicated professionals whose "life work" might include countering a senator's argument over the location of the Panama Canal, fighting against compound locomotives, describing a Ford for an audience of both mechanics and chauffeurs, and providing instructions on retail accounting systems. A 1917 text for such a course, *Writing for the Trade Press,* emphasizes the opportunities offered by these professional publications:

The writer who has mastered the technique of literary construction and who is willing to go into the practical work connected with some line of business has an opportunity to become so superior a trade paper worker so as to be able to reach the top in that line of work when the same amount of effort and ability might not make him even a recognized regular contributor to a literary publication. (Farrington 8)

Technical and Business Writing in the English Department

As journalism schools became less oriented toward "non-professional" instruction, English departments increasingly provided the technical writing classes taken by students in engineering, agriculture, business, and other fields. These English offerings usually gave more attention to basic skills and to letter and report writing and less to journalistic style and article formats. Although the new courses were placed at the advanced level, they were not always taken by advanced students, ones who planned to be writers, but by every type of technical major, students required to be there. Without a motivated student population or a definite connection to a career, these courses did not immediately lead to a new professional writing program as had the first offerings in creative writing and journalism.

Some "English for engineering" courses reflected the general education goals of English departments—and of industry critics like Horace See and Oberlin Smith. After a first semester on basic composition, students in writing classes at MIT taught by Frank Aydelotte, an English professor who later became president of Swarthmore College, considered the following questions:

What is the difference between a trade and a profession? What is the meaning of the professional spirit? What should be the position of the engineer in society in this new era of the manufacture of power—that of hired expert or that of leader and adviser? Is the function of the engineer to direct only the material forces of nature, or also human forces? . . . What is the aim of engineering education? . . . What is the relation between pure science and applied? What is the relation of science to literature? (Mann 63–64)

To judge the possible answers, students read engineering reports, scientific articles by Huxley and Tyndall, and literary essays by Arnold, Newman, Carlyle, and Ruskin and wrote their own responses. Aydelotte's text *English and Engineering* (1917) provides pieces by Ruskin, Carlyle, Emerson, Whitman, and other authors to help students examine the effects of technology and progress. At the University of Wisconsin, Karl Young taught similar courses concerning engineering and society. At Minnesota, Charles Washburn Nichols offered a half-year freshman course in which engineering students studied four Shakespeare plays, along with technical reports and articles, to broaden their understanding of human motivations, a "professional need":

> The typical engineering Freshman has an interesting, active mind, but a very narrow one. His eye has been so steadily fixed on his future profession that he has failed to see the need, even the professional need, of a broad contact with life, of a sympathetic knowledge of human nature. Literature, and particularly dramatic literature, where character is unfolded in action, gives any student a contact with life. (366)

Nichols noted that the engineering student enjoyed studying plot because "he likes to see how things are put together" (367).

Other texts and classes offered engineering students another possibility: a writing course that considered engineering as a business career. Some business schools adopted Edwin Lewis's *Business English* (1911), but his primary audience, as he states in his preface, was college engineering students, including those in correspondence courses:

> This work grew out of teaching English to college men who were beginning their studies in Engineering. It seemed for various reasons desirable to give such students—along with their work in pure literature and technical English—some instruction in English as adapted to buying and selling, advertising and correspondence. (i)

His book contains chapters on punctuation, grammar, and diction as well as business letters, managerial reports, and advertising copy. The second volume of Carl A. Naether's 1930 text *A Course in English for Engineers,* entitled *The Engineer's Professional and Business Writing,* reflects a similar emphasis. His co-author was George Francis Richardson, who had taught composition to engineering students at Missouri and Texas. This volume covers many types of business letters, such as inquiries, orders, applications, and claims, and also gives two chapters to proposals and reports. In the first chapter, Naether defends his teaching of business letter writing to engineering students by arguing that many engineering graduates take jobs as "superintendents, inspectors, foremen, job demonstrators, experimental men, and, in their offices, cost accountants, time-study men, sales engineers, and office managers" (Naether and Richardson II, 3). He also maintains that field engineers will need letter-writing skills throughout their careers. By the 1930s, many schools had business writing courses for engineering students: Carnegie University, for example, required engineering management majors to take Business Communication; Purdue offered Business Writing: Engineering Applications as an elective for juniors and seniors in the engineering school (Fountain 52, 59).

Most of the new courses in English for engineering, however, did not emphasize general education or business prose, but instead taught basic writing skills and engineering formats. The first widely used text devoted to this type of technical writing instruction was published in 1908 by engineering editor T. A. Rickard. His *A Guide to Technical Writing,* which had been intended as a desk reference, mostly concerns usage, with chapters on abbreviations, numbers, hyphens, relative pronouns, titles, and page specifications aimed at helping engineers to "write simply and clearly; be accurate and careful" (13). As editor for the *Engineering and Mining Journal,* he had become dismayed over the prevailing tendency toward technical jargon and had begun writing speeches and journal articles advocating better writing, as he noted in his autobiography. His guide was an extension of that effort, "to preach the need for care in writing" both to established engineers and to "the younger men" (*Retrospect* 118, 121).

Texts by English professors—who generally had no technical training or experience—quickly followed, often re-creating the instruction and assignments from their first technical writing classes. Seeing their mission as preparing students for a career of article, report, and letter writing, these teachers did not join the debate from creative writing and journalism over whether the writer was "born" or could be "made." If the authors defend the need for training at all, they do so without mentioning any philosophical doubts:

> Nowadays reports play a large part in public and corporate affairs. As a natural consequence, an increasing number of men and women must know how to write them. . . . This book, which applies certain principles of composition and rhetoric to the special field of the report, is intended to be helpful to those writers who are either inexperienced or less effective than they would like to be. (Gaum and Graves iii)

Most textbook writers, like Homer Watt, simply assert the need for good writing and writing instruction—as "a truth which all experienced engineers recognize." Their only fight was with fellow faculty who thought that this necessary training shouldn't be part of the English department's curriculum.

Unlike the new books on journalism and creative writing, these first texts were heavily influenced by the freshman composition paradigm. They rely on the forms of discourse, paragraph rules, and grammar instruction, perhaps because they were intended for a wider range of students, many of whom might need basic work, and because they were written by English professors with little technical experience who were trying to make the new courses seem acceptable to their colleagues. *The Theory and Practice of Technical Writing*, published in 1911 by Samuel Chandler Earle, an English instructor at Tufts College who later became a professor in the engineering school, grew out of his courses in "engineering English" begun in 1904. He divides technical exposition into narrative, descriptive, and directive prose. Homer Watt's *The Composition of Technical Papers* (1917) includes chapters on correspondence and reports as well as technical description, exposition of processes, exposition of ideas, essay and paragraph structure, and sentence grammar. Watt taught in the English department at Wisconsin and then at New York University. In *English Applied in Technical Writing* (1926), Clyde W. Park, an English professor in the College of Commerce and Engineering at the University of Cincinnati, concentrates on paragraphing, organization, word use, grammar, and the writer's literary background.

As textbooks multiplied and as more students enrolled in technical writing courses, textbook authors began trying to modify the forms of discourse approach to more accurately represent technical communication. *The Preparation of Reports: Engineering, Scientific, Administrative* (1924), a text by Roy P. Baker, head of the English department at Rensselaer, considers the characteristics of technical reports from the fourteenth century onward, divides the current types into information, examination, recommendation, progress, and research reports, and furnishes over 60 professional examples of these categories. Baker's text had gone through five editions by 1953. *Report Writing* (1929), by Carl G. Gaum, an extension professor at Rutgers, and Harold F. Graves, an English professor at Penn State, surveys the forms of discourse, but then provides separate chapters on periodic, progress, examination, and recommendation reports. In *The Engineer's Manual of English* (1933), W. O. Sypherd, an English professor at Delaware, and Sharon Brown, an English professor at Brown, discuss clear style and organization and then turn to information, examination, and research reports as well as types of engineering letters, technical journal articles, bulletins, and specifications, providing professional examples of each genre.

Besides various divisions of report and article types, books published in each decade after 1910 incorporated increasing amounts of material on audience and style. Earle's text from 1911 contains examples of engineering writing addressed to an audience of engineering specialists. Baker's *The Preparation of Reports* (1924) contrasts the purpose, form, and language of reports written by an employee for the employer, by an expert consultant for a client, and by an independent researcher for a journal or bulletin. In *English Applied in Technical Writing* (1926), Clyde Park discusses specialists, educated persons without expert knowledge, and general readers as possible audiences to be reached through technical, semitechnical, and nontechnical writing styles. In *Report Writing* (1929), Gaum and Graves also describe the rhetorical situation of a technician addressing an executive or decision-maker who might have little technical training. In *The Preparation of Engineering Reports* (1935), Thomas Agg and Walter Foster, both of Iowa State's engineering school, include a chapter on using graphic elements—diagrams, charts, and graphs—to convince various types of readers (Maher 55–61).

Technical writing courses following these books' approach— with the focus on forms of discourse and correct grammar and increasingly also on reports addressed to various audiences— began appearing by 1916 in English departments at a number of schools, including Tufts, the University of Cincinnati, MIT, the University of Kansas, and Rensselaer (Connors, "Rise of Technical Writing Instruction" 333). In 1918, a survey conducted for the Society for the Promotion of Engineering Education showed that most engineering students were still taking only freshman composition:

> As regards electives, the situation is not so satisfactory as it might appear. For instance, nine schools out of twenty-six offer no elective courses in English; the remaining seventeen in one group offer electives in one or more of the following courses: English literature, business English, advanced English, and public speaking. Only two institutions report many takers for these elective courses. (Mann 179–80)

A 1932 report, however, revealed a drastic change: "The Freshman composition is all but universal. An advanced course in technical, report, or business writing is required in nearly half of the institutions; and this is placed most commonly in the Senior year, although not infrequently it is in the Junior year" (Creek and McKee 823). A 1938 report showed that 76 of 117 institutional members of the Society for the Promotion of Engineering Education then offered 93 different technical writing courses, with 67 of them being required in at least one department of an engineering school. Forty-three of the 76 institutions were state universities or state A&M colleges; nineteen had English departments within the engineering college (Fountain 45, 64–67, 70). English professors and instructors usually offered engineering English; engineers rarely entered the university to teach writing as had creative writers and journalists.

The steady growth of engineering English never carried over to agriculture. Harry R. O'Brien of the Oklahoma Agricultural and Mechanical College maintained in 1914 that no effort had been made to teach expository writing concerning agricultural topics, no magazine articles and conference sessions had been devoted to the topic, and no textbook had been written for agricultural English. He recognized that agricultural journalism courses, mostly concerned with training writing specialists, would not fulfill the needs of most students (472). At that time, a few engineering writing courses enrolled agriculture students. Sara Harbarger, an English professor at Ohio State University, described her text *English for Engineers* (1928) as an edited version of materials from her class enrolling engineering, agriculture, and pharmacy students. In the 1920s, a few universities also instituted special courses for agriculture students. Texas A&M's English department, for example, offered a sophomore-level course, English Composition, "to give the student practice in writing themes and reports on subjects related to his studies in agriculture" (Texas Agricultural and Mechanical College, Catalogue 1920–21 166). Penn State had a special writing course for students in a two-year agricultural program. At the University of Minnesota/St. Paul, the Department of Rhetoric offered advanced courses in technical writing for agriculture students. Roy Baker stated in the preface to his 1924 *The Preparation of Reports* that his text would be appropriate for such classes. But few agriculture programs initiated advanced writing courses; they relied instead on the training provided in freshman composition and in their technical classes.

Developing at a time when advanced training for writers was becoming an accepted notion, business programs immediately drew on the English department's writing, if not business, expertise. At the University of Illinois, Thomas Arkle Clark, who held an endowed chair in rhetoric, taught business writing for 11 years, followed by Thacher Howland Guild, who taught nineteenth-century literature and directed the University Theatre. The 1902 course description read: "Business Writing—business correspondence, the making of summaries and abstracts, advertising, proofreading, and preparation of manuscripts for the press" (Weeks 207).

New York University's School of Commerce, Accounts, and Finance established a business writing course in 1906, taught by the dean of the college, Joseph French Johnson, who had instituted the journalism program at the University of Pennsylvania. George Burton Hotchkiss took over the course in 1908. A graduate of Yale, he was an instructor of English at Beloit College from 1906 to 1908 and at New York University from 1908 to 1911; he then moved into the School of Commerce and became head of its business English department in 1916 and later head of its marketing department. At Wisconsin, Edward Hall Gardner, assistant professor of English and later a professor of business administration, taught the first business writing course around 1905.

As business schools extended their curricula, some began to add more business writing courses. In 1907 Illinois split its basic business writing course into two semesters: "The first semester will be devoted to business correspondence with practice in incidental writing, summaries, etc. The second semester will include advertising, preparation of copy, and proofreading." In 1913, Harrison McJohnston, a new instructor in salesmanship and business English at Illinois, instituted two additional courses: "Sales Correspondence—the economic and psychological principles underlying successful sales letter writing; planning the letter sales campaign; the form of the followup letters; analysis of markets, etc." and "Summarizing and Abstracting—summarizing, briefing, and making reports; abstracts of correspondence on file; summarizing of commercial and economic data" (Weeks 205–07).

To develop these writing courses, universities tried to enlist, and hold onto, teachers with business experience, even though these hires faced opposition from other English department faculty. Herbert L. Creek studied shorthand and typing, failed to prosper in a business job, worked as a school teacher, and then entered graduate school so that he could get a college teaching job; he was asked to teach business writing at the University of Illinois, he wrote much later, because "somebody remembered that I had once been a stenographer" (6). Harrison McJohnston came to Illinois in 1913 after teaching economics at Ohio State and working as a copywriter, sales correspondent, and editor at *System* and *Printer's Ink*. Of McJohnston's problems in the English department, Creek wrote:

> He was not of the academic type and never had much support from the administration of the English Department. I feel reasonably certain, for example, that Professor Sherman [Stuart Pratt Sherman, noted literary critic and head of the English department] did not particularly like him and would have preferred to have a literary scholar who knew enough about business to teach the course. (Weeks 205)

McJohnston left Illinois in 1918 to work for a publishing company in Chicago. Creek commented on this departure: "But soon a business concern lured him away with a salary of a hundred dollars a week—a fabulous sum in those days and probably more than the head of the department of English was getting" (6).

For these early business writing courses, no college textbooks were available, but teachers could draw from other printed materials. After the Civil War, as prosperous merchants and factory owners sought a social status equal to their income, etiquette books that contained sections on writing to relatives, casual friends, intimate friends of the opposite sex, employers, and city officials became popular. By the 1880s and 1890s, some of these books contained fairly thorough treatments of application letters, collection letters, letters of inquiry, and letters conveying good and bad news. After the turn of the century, complete books on the etiquette of business correspondence began appearing, which offered little instruction but instead relied on models (Denton 88–89). J. Willis Westlake, professor of English literature at the State Normal School in Millersville, Pennsylvania, wrote such a guide, *How to Write Letters: A Manual of Correspondence,* "designed, both in matter and method, to meet the wants, not only of schools of various grades, but also of private learners and of society at large" through its coverage of letter structures and punctuation (3–4). Books intended for commercial high schools, such as *Commercial Correspondence* and *Postal Information* (1904) by Carl Lewis Altmaier of the Drexel Institute, and others written for home study courses, such as George Hotchkiss's 12 pamphlets entitled *Business English*, could also be used by the college teacher.

From his home study books, Hotchkiss developed one of the first influential college-level business writing textbooks, *Business English: Principles and Practice* (1916), coauthored with Celia Anne Drew. Although this book does not mention the forms of discourse, it does involve some features of freshman composition: instruction concerning grammar; unity, coherence, and emphasis as they apply to the sentence, paragraph, and longer piece; and clearness and force of style. This book also considers new "principles" of business writing: the influential "Five C's" (completeness, consideration, clarity, courtesy, and correctness), the "you" attitude created by considering the character and needs of the reader, and the requirements of specific formats, such as claims, collections, and sales letters, advertisements, and reports. Edward Hall Gardner's *Effective Business Letters* from 1915 contains instruction and examples to teach students about letters intended to give information, order goods, give notice of shipments, sell products, and collect debts. In one short chapter on principles of effective writing, Gardner also covers unity, coherence, and emphasis, appropriate word choices, and the proper alternation of short and long sentences.

Additional information on business letter formats and audience analysis could be found in *How to Write Business Letters*, a college edition of *How to Write Letters That Win*, part of a "how-to" series written by the editors at System Company Publishers. The revised version, which was published in 1916 and went through 18 printings by 1929, was done by Walter Kay Smart, head of the English department of Armour Institute of Technology and lecturer on business correspondence in the School of Commerce at Northwestern University. The book provides formats for applications, inquiries, orders, adjustments, collections, sales, and other types of letters. It extends

Hotchkiss's presentation of the "you" attitude through an audience analysis process: writers who must address distant parties, Smart suggests, should envision typical individuals from "certain broad classes" defined by profession, section of the country, and other information, test trial letters on members of those groups, and then write the actual correspondence with the resulting formulations in mind. Smart frequently makes comparisons to speaking, suggesting that the reader approach the client by talking "to him as if he were at your desk" (9–10). On facing pages, he gives examples of letters that lack and that contain a direct "you" appeal to the reader's needs. This note, for example, follows one faulty letter:

> Nothing robs a letter of directness more than a lack of the "you" element. This man tries to sell a pair of shoes by talking not about the prospect and his needs but about himself and his product. Note the prevalence of "our" and "we" in every paragraph. Half of the words are mere machinery. (152)

To conclude the final chapter on audience, Smart again concentrates on the primacy of human needs: "A good salesman never mentions the selling end of his game; he emphasizes the buying point. . . . You may think it selfish, but I repeat that the nearest subject to me is me. The most interesting theme with you is you. It is a human trait—as infallible as a physical law" (155). To illustrate its principles, the book provides 1,200 letters from manufacturers.

With more texts and teachers arriving, business writing became an accepted part of business and English departments, at the University of Illinois, New York University, Northwestern, and Wisconsin and then at many other schools such as DePaul, Nebraska, and Southern California. Over half of all business schools required a business writing class by 1930 (Russell 127). In these classes, offered either as requirements or as electives, students learned about business letter formats, audience analysis, clear style, and correct grammar as well as report writing and advertising. Because this curriculum resembled technical writing, although usually business courses involved less emphasis on reports and the forms of discourse and more on letters and audience appeals, the two genres were never completely distinct; some schools offered business and technical writing as one course. But because sales seemed markedly different from other office communications, separate classes concerning advertising and ad copy writing were instituted in some English departments and, more frequently, in business and communications schools.

Technical and business writing enrollments grew after World War II and again after the Sputnik educational crisis, as Americans faced the communications needs created by technological and corporate growth. As engineering and business enrollments increased, so did enrollments in the writing courses intended as electives or requirements for technical majors. By the 1950s, many corporations opened separate writing divisions, thus creating job opportunities for specialists in technical writing and editing. As in journalism and creative writing, each decade brought less reliance on set formats. Texts began to focus on the rhetorical principles of scientific and business prose—on the writing process, audience analysis, and readability—as well as on reports, letters, manuals, proposals, and other forms. These newer books, like Gordon Mill's *Technical Writing* (1954) and Houp and Pearsall's *Reporting Technical Information* (1968), and the classes using them, frequently reached the larger "technical" audience of students in architecture, pharmacy, home economics, physical therapy, and other fields.

This growth, however, didn't establish a clear career in teaching technical or business writing or a secure place for such courses in the curriculum. While journalism and creative writing programs quickly developed graduate degrees to train their own staffs, advanced degrees in technical and business writing were slower in coming, with few programs available before the 1970s. Into that decade, English professors found that specializing in technical or business writing might have a detrimental impact on their careers; thus instructors or teaching assistants were often drafted to do this "second-class" work (Connors, "Rise of Technical Writing Instruction" 338–40, 344–45). The professors and technical writers who joined business and engineering schools did not find an easier road to acceptance and promotion there. The courses' audience continued to waver since business and industry never solidly backed the requirement of training in writing for all new hires and the position of technical writing specialist had not yet become widely accepted. Thus these advanced writing courses were often the odd part of a technical or English degree, with no group dedicated to their success. It was not until the 1980s that committed teachers, organizations like the Society for Technical Communication, and journals like the *Journal of Business Communication* and the *Journal of Technical Writing and Communication* helped improve the status of technical and business writing programs, teachers, and graduates.

Because technical and business writing teachers have only recently obtained a fairly secure status, they have traditionally been allied with other composition teachers within English departments. But their status change is leading to greater separation, as can be seen in separate teaching positions, conferences, and degrees. Growth is also causing teachers of technical and business writing to separate from one another, often into different departments. Thus these teachers, even though they share the same debates over formats, the writing process, and career preparation, and even though they have much to offer all writing students, may become as isolated from advanced and freshman composition teachers and from each other as they already are from teachers of journalism and creative writing. For these writing specializations as for the others, growth has its costs.

8

Conclusion

Although the divisions of professional writing quickly separated, with different staffs, texts, and programs, they shared a similar history. They all began around 1900 as experimental offerings in English departments, as attempts to meet the need for additional writing training after freshman composition and to respond to the interest in professional education. They all began as reactions to a new college curriculum in which most students would become versed in a specific discipline, but not in writing. While the first teachers and textbook authors were primarily English department literature professors, soon other teachers were brought in from the writing professions, with perhaps less academic training and no teaching experience but with practical knowledge of the discipline. They introduced courses that offered less general work on style and essay structure, but more experience with the specific type of professional writing.

These first teachers generally avoided the college forms of classification, definition, and comparison, but they set up their own format-based syllabi. In poetry classes, students completed assignment sequences of sonnets, sestets, and quatrains; in short story classes, they learned to emphasize setting, theme, character, and action. Journalism students studied the appropriate formats for reporting political events, fires, accidents, and society news. Technical and business writing students moved through different types of letters and reports.

As the formats began to seem like unrealistic exercises, especially to the professional writers entering the colleges as teachers, further change occurred: creative writing students began participating in workshops centered on their own projects. Journalism students took newsroom classes in which they turned out editions of campus and local papers. Technical and business writing students studied the actual rhetorical situations involved in proposals, manuals, and other types of business discourse. As these writing teachers broke away from traditional methods of teaching composition, their classes began to seem like an anomaly in the English department. And the teachers themselves did not fit in there since they rarely met the increasing requirements for graduate education and scholarly publication.

Because of this antagonism—and the new courses concerning newspaper business and history—journalism programs soon were housed in separate departments and colleges. With support from the American press and a clear connection to available employment, journalism instruction did not have to remain in English departments as an awkward stepchild. The other divisions of professional writing, however, had no clear mandate for separate growth. Creative writing teachers were involved with literature; their classes did not lead to the employment opportunities that journalism training created. Technical and business writing teachers never secured enough support from engineering, agriculture, or business schools to develop as a separate unit. These three types of professional writing teachers generally remained as peripheral members of English departments.

By the 1920s, advanced writing instruction was well established if not totally accepted. Even during the Depression, most schools maintained their offerings. Individual colleges discontinued some courses, as Michigan did in 1930 after Fred Newton Scott retired and the rhetoric professors reentered the English department, but the number of advanced writing courses grew during each decade.

A boost for all types of professional writing instruction oc-curred after World War II. The war showed the importance of technology and communications, and thus of technical writing, business writing, and journalism. In the 1940s, many new jour-nalism programs were instituted, especially at the rapidly grow-ing state schools such as Tennessee, Florida, Wyoming, Maine, and Maryland. Technical writing courses entered many colleges during that period to prepare students for modern communica-tions; engineering students continued to take at least one ad-vanced writing course while some English majors began to specialize in technical writing and editing. The success of these courses also led to a broader audience of students from chem-istry, pharmacy, and home economics (Connors, "Rise of Tech-nical Writing Instruction," 330–42).

The GI's returning in large numbers to American universities also created a new interest in modern American literature and in creative writing as these older adults looked to imaginative prose to help them analyze their own experiences. English de-partments offered more twentieth-century literature, especially courses on the novel, than they had before the war. With pros-perity, more schools extended invitations to well-known writers to join their staffs. The summer writing conference and writers' institute became common by 1950.

Events of subsequent decades caused growth spurts through-out the professional writing curriculum. The Sputnik educa-tional crisis of the 1950s and the Korean war boosted American instruction in science—and scientific writing. The protest movements of the 1960s caused greater interest in the self-expression of creative writing: this period witnessed more writ-ers on campus, more creative workshops at every level, and the rapid development of B.F.A. and M.F.A. programs. The Water-gate scandal and the celebrity of Woodward and Bernstein brought legions of students to journalism, more than could find jobs. During each decade, each of the divisions of profes-sional writing spawned new courses to meet the demand caused by larger student populations: instruction in television and film writing entered creative writing and journalism programs; jour-nalism developed into "communications" with new writing courses concerning television news, film, advertising, and public relations; technical writing instruction increased with new information on reports, user documentation, and editing; business writing expanded into oral and written communications and into sales and advertising courses.

Beginning in the 1960s, the new interest in rhetoric in English departments had an impact on the general advanced composition courses. As teachers reevaluated the current/traditional paradigm of the freshman program, they also had to consider whether that approach was best for advanced students. Rhetoric specialists who might not be able to transform the institutionalized freshman courses found more latitude in the few sections of general advanced composition. Teachers began to focus on the writing process, the nonfiction essay, library research, expressionistic writing, and critical thinking, a large group of possibilities that made the courses more challenging but not more clearly defined. Modern rhetorical theory also influenced instruction in technical writing, creating more emphasis on the writing process and on audience analysis, bringing to the discipline well-trained writing professionals who were not awaiting their chance to escape to literature courses.

In the 1970s and 1980s, advanced writing teachers were also influenced by the writing-across-the-curriculum movement, especially by theories concerning discourse communities and writing as an aid to learning. This emphasis on the rhetorical situation and formats of writing in the humanities and sciences informed new advanced classes offered in the English department. Writing specialists also helped to create "writing emphasis" courses taught by workshop-trained teachers from the disciplines. This development had little impact on established programs in professional writing, although it did divert some students, like those in pharmacy and chemistry, from the traditional technical writing classes.

The increase in advanced writing courses in each decade occurred along with continuing debates on how, and whether, to teach writing. In 1890 and 1900, this debate concerned whether advanced writing training was appropriate, whether students instead should work and learn as apprentices, whether a writer could be "made" by any method. By 1920, some critics accepted the concept of instruction and instead debated the efficacy of various teaching methods. When the classroom emphasis shifted from formats to the actual work environment of the newsroom or writers' group, teachers were praised for providing more realistic training and criticized for being too practical, too makeshift. While these practicum courses brought high enrollments, they were labeled as no more than college apprenticeships, and not very good apprenticeships in such a restricted environment and with only one experienced mentor. Each decade after World War II brought switches back and forth. Some creative writing teachers put more emphasis on critical reading, creating assignment and course sequences to ensure that students knew the history and techniques of the genre before launching into their own work. Some switched back to a freer workshop model during the 1960s and then changed again in subsequent decades. After World War II, many journalism programs ended their ties with local papers and remade the campus paper into a voluntary activity, giving more attention in class to principles of research and style. Some later reinstated newsroom classes because their graduates seemed inadequately prepared for jobs. Some technical writing classes began to deemphasize formats and give more time to principles of persuasion and the requirements of various audiences, while others created sequences based on newer forms such as proposals and manuals. Teachers in all of these writing disciplines continued to ask whether their classes were providing better training than years in the world, on the job; whether they were too theoretical or too practical; whether they contained too much reading, lecture, discussion, or writing; whether they gave too much attention to the authors' processes or their products; whether the individual courses made a coherent sequence; whether the major took up too much of the college curriculum or too little. Conflict also continued concerning the proper academic credentials and publication expectations for these faculty hires.

These similar questions, and similar growth patterns, have not led the advanced writing divisions to seek answers together. Our students now write for periodicals, magazines, newsletters, and brochures that contain science, business, entertainment, and every other kind of writing in scholarly and personal styles; even the most technical articles involve more than informative discourse. The employment categories have begun to blur; any writing student could now profit from a combination of what we have taught in our separate corners and decided on as our separate answers. The professional discourse and teaching experiences of rhetoric, advanced composition, creative writing, journalism, technical writing, and business writing need to blur also.

Many English department writing programs have begun recognizing the power of a more eclectic writing program and have extended their older creative writing degrees to include technical and business writing, feature writing, autobiography and biography, research, and other models of advanced composition. Over 300 schools now have an English department writing major or minor that combines literature and an array of advanced writing courses. At many schools the older advanced composition courses focusing on general or "transferable" skills, to use Ross Winterowd's terminology, seem to be moving into two divisions, with one placed at the sophomore and one at the senior level. Thus courses in expository, research, or argumentative skills, along with basic classes on grammar and style, might initiate the student to the program. At a middle level might be the array of "local" or specific genre courses, focusing on writing for journalism, business, law, technical fields, and other types of discourse, including writing-across-the-curriculum offerings from various departments. Within this group might be some sequencing, like two levels of news writing or technical writing, along with single courses in legal writing, magazine writing, and other genres. At the highest level might be a second group of transferable skills courses focusing on the writing process and revision, the publication process, word processing, and individual projects. Internships might also occur at this senior level. Students might choose a number of courses from each level, with the largest percentage given to the local skills courses that suit the students' career interests.

Penn State University, for example, has an introductory-level course on the process of writing and the relation of fiction to nonfiction, a transferable skills course. Students can also take local skills courses emphasizing poetry and fiction, nonfiction and article writing, biographical writing, writing in social sciences, humanities, technical, and business fields, television script writing and radio drama writing, science writing, and technical writing and editing. The senior-level courses include two transferable courses, Problems of Style and The Editing Process. At Loyola University in New Orleans, students start with a course focusing on primary and secondary research. Then they may choose among courses on poetry, fiction, script writing, reviewing, technical writing, writing for the law, and writing for international audiences. The senior-level courses emphasize longer projects, word processing and desktop publishing, and professional experience.

Other schools have installed prerequisite systems to formalize the students' involvement in several genres. At North Carolina State University, the sophomore-level Introduction to Prose Writing is a prerequisite for the newswriting, poetry, and fiction courses. Advanced Nonfiction, a workshop for students who want to publish magazine articles or nonfiction books, has newswriting as a prerequisite. At Arizona State, professional writing has an intermediate creative writing course as a prerequisite.

Writing-across-the-curriculum programs have also brought teachers and students into contact with various genres of professional writing. At California State University, Fullerton, for example, students can choose among courses like Writing in the Visual Arts, Geographical Writing, and Philosophical Argument and Writing. Although the primary audience for these writing-emphasis courses is students in those disciplines, these courses are also helpful to English majors planning to be writers. At the University of Tennessee, similarly, a course designed for science students who are writing master's theses and technical articles can also be taken by English majors who serve as writing coaches to the other students.

These curricular innovations signal positive changes in our writing curricula. Within the English department, we need to be more aware of the strengths of all writing teachers and of the instruction they can offer our students. We need to discuss the appropriate curriculum for a major or minor in writing and to arrange possible course sequences that involve all types of writing courses. Such efforts might be extended through combined writing majors involving English, journalism, business, and other departments, a harder decision to make given campus divisions but an important one for reinstituting a dialogue among teachers and for training our students. Just through down-the-hall and across-campus talk, we can eliminate the current animosities and begin to understand what our colleagues are doing. And we can do so on our own terms, for the greater stability and effectiveness of all divisions, not in forced response to mandates that may stem from the cost-accounting cutbacks facing higher education in the 1990s. We might suggest that our students take writing courses from other departments, perhaps as electives, and then we might move toward team-teaching, joint hires, joint conferences, and combined writing majors. We have much in common and much to learn from one another.

Works Cited

Adams, Katherine H., and John L. Adams. "Advanced Composition: Where Did It Come From? Where Is It Going?" *Teaching Advanced Composition: Why and How*. Ed. Katherine H. Adams and John L. Adams. Portsmouth, NH: Heinemann, 1991. 3–15.

———. "The Paradox Within: Origins of the Current/ Traditional Paradigm." *Rhetoric Society Quarterly* 17 (1987): 421–31.

"The Advanced Course in Expository Writing: Aims, Texts, and Methods." *College Composition and Communication* 9 (1958): 165–67.

Agg, Thomas R., and Walter L. Foster. *The Preparation of Engineering Reports*. New York: McGraw, 1935.

Altmaier, Carl Lewis. *Commercial Correspondence and Postal Information*. New York: Macmillan, 1904.

Announcement of the Department of English 1894–95, ts. Pusey Library, Harvard U.

Annual Reports of the President and Treasurer of Harvard College, 1890–91. Cambridge: Harvard College, 1892.

Applebee, Arthur N. *Tradition and Reform in the Teaching of English: A History*. Urbana: NCTE, 1974.

Archer, William. *Play-Making: A Manual of Craftsmanship*. Boston: Small, Maynard, 1912.

Arnold, Matthew. *Culture and Anarchy*. London: Smith, Elder, 1869.

Aydelotte, Frank. *English and Engineering*. New York: McGraw, 1917.

Baker, George Pierce. "Barrett Wendell (1855–1921)." *Harvard Graduates' Magazine* 29 (1921): 571–76.

———. *Dramatic Technique*. Boston: Houghton, 1919.

———. "The 47 Workshop." *Century* 101 (1921): 417–25.

———. "The 47 Workshop." *Quarterly Journal of Speech Education* 5 (1919): 185–95.

Baker, Harry T. "Journalism and Creative Writing." *Journalism Bulletin* 3 (1926): 37–40.

Baker, Ray Palmer. *The Preparation of Reports: Engineering, Scientific, Administrative.* New York: Ronald, 1924.

Barrett, Charles Raymond. *Short Story Writing.* New York: Doubleday, 1900.

Battle, Kemp P. *History of the University of North Carolina.* Vol. 1. Raleigh: Edwards and Broughton, 1907.

———. *History of the University of North Carolina.* Vol. 2. Raleigh: Edwards and Broughton, 1912.

Berlin, James A. *Writing Instruction in Nineteenth-Century American Colleges.* Carbondale: Southern Illinois UP, 1984.

Billier, W. B. de. English 12, Themes on Student Life, 1886–87, ms. Pusey Library, Harvard U.

Bledstein, Burton J. *The Culture of Professionalism.* New York: Norton, 1976.

Bleyer, Willard Grosvenor. *Types of News Writing.* Boston: Houghton, 1916.

Bohman, George V. "Rhetorical Practice in Colonial America." *A History of Speech Education in America.* Ed. Karl R. Wallace. New York: Appleton, 1954. 60–79.

Breitenbach, Harold P. *The Value of English to the Practicing Engineer.* Contributions to Rhetorical Theory 7. Ed. Fred Newton Scott. Ann Arbor: Library Printing, 1906.

Brittin, Norman A. *Edna St. Vincent Millay.* Rev. ed. Boston: Twayne, 1982.

Brooks, Van Wyck. *New England: Indian Summer, 1865–1915.* New York: Dutton, 1940.

Broome, Edwin C. *A Historical and Critical Discussion of College Admission Requirements.* Columbia University Contributions to Philosophy, Psychology and Education 11. New York: Columbia U, 1903.

Broun, Heywood. "Nipping the Budding Playwright in the Bud." *Vanity Fair* 13 (October 1919): 63.

Brown, John Mason. "The Four Georges: G. P. Baker at Work." *Theatre Arts Monthly* 17 (July 1933): 537–51.

Brown, Rollo. *Dean Briggs.* New York: Harper, 1926.

Brubacher, J. S., and W. Rudy. *Higher Education in Transition: A History of American Colleges and Universities, 1636–1976.* 3rd ed. New York: Harper, 1976.

Buck, Gertrude. "'Make-Believe Grammar.'" *School Review* 17 (1909): 21–33.

Burdett, C. H. English 12, Themes on Student Life, 1886–87, ms. Pusey Library, Harvard U.

Butts, R. Freeman. "European Models for American Higher Education (1636–1860)." *Viewpoints* 47.5 (1971): 19–43.

Calvert, Monte A. *The Mechanical Engineer in America, 1830–1910.* Baltimore: Johns Hopkins UP, 1967.

Camp, Eugene M. *Journalists: Born or Made?* Philadelphia: Philadelphia Social Science Association, 1888.

Capen, Samuel P. *The Management of Universities.* Buffalo: Foster and Stewart, 1953.

Carhart, Henry S. "The Twentieth Century Engineer." *Addresses to Engineering Students.* Ed. J. A. L. Waddell and John Harrington. 2nd ed. Kansas City, MO: Waddell and Harrington, 1912. 209–18.

Carruth, William Herbert. *Verse Writing.* New York: Macmillan, 1917.

Cashman, Sean Dennis. *America in the Age of the Titans: The Progressive Era and World War I.* New York: New York UP, 1988.

Cheit, Earl F. *The Useful Arts and the Liberal Tradition.* New York: McGraw, 1975.

Chittenden, Russell Henry. "The Story of the Founding of the Sheffield Scientific School." *Inventors and Engineers of Old New Haven.* Ed. Richard Shelton Kirby. New Haven: New Haven Colony Historical Society, 1939.

Clyde, Thomas. English 12, Themes on Student Life, 1886–87, ms. Pusey Library, Harvard U.

Cole, Richard R. "Much Better Than Yesterday, and Still Brighter Tomorrow." *Journalism Educator* 40.3 (1985): 4–8.

Connors, Robert J. "Handbooks: History of a Genre." *Rhetoric Society Quarterly* 13 (1983): 87–98.

———. "Mechanical Correctness as a Focus in Composition Instruction." *College Composition and Communication* 36 (1985): 61–72.

———. "The Rise and Fall of the Modes of Discourse." *College Composition and Communication* 32 (1981): 444–55.

———. "The Rise of Technical Writing Instruction in America." *Journal of Technical Writing and Communication* 12 (1982): 329–52.

Conrad, Lawrence H. *Teaching Creative Writing*. New York: Appleton, 1937.

Cooper, James Fenimore. *The American Democrat*. 1838. New York: Knopf, 1931.

Copeland, Charles Townsend, and H. M. Rideout. *Freshman English and Theme-Correcting in Harvard College*. New York: Silver, 1901.

Counts, George S. *The Senior High School Curriculum*. Chicago: Univ. of Chicago, 1926.

Cowan, Louise. *The Fugitive Group: A Literary History*. Baton Rouge: Louisiana State UP, 1959.

Cowley, Malcolm. *Exile's Return*. 1934. New York: Viking, 1951.

———. *The Literary Situation*. New York: Viking, 1954.

Craig, Virginia J. *The Teaching of High School English*. New York: Longmans, 1930.

Crawford, Nelson Antrim, and Charles Elkins Rogers. *Agricultural Journalism*. New York: Knopf, 1926.

Creek, Herbert L. "How I Became an Expert on Business Letter Writing." *ABWA Bulletin* 17 (1952): 5–7.

Creek, Herbert L., and J. H. McKee. "English in Colleges in Engineering." *English Journal* 21 (1932): 818–28.

Daley, John M. *Georgetown University: Origin and Early Years*. Washington: Georgetown UP, 1957.

Davidson, Donald. *Southern Writers in the Modern World*. Athens: U of Georgia P, 1958.

Denney, Joseph V. *Two Problems in Composition-Teaching*. Contributions to Rhetorical Theory 3. Ed. Fred Newton Scott. Ann Arbor: U of Michigan, n.d.

Denton, L. W. "The Etiquette of American Business Correspondence." *Studies in the History of Business Writing*. Ed. George H. Douglas and Herbert W. Hildebrandt. Urbana: Association for Business Communication, 1985. 87–95.

Dickens, Charles. *American Notes and Pictures from Italy. 1842 and 1846.* London: Oxford UP, 1978.

Digest of Education Statistics. 25th ed. Washington: US Department of Education, 1989.

Doty, Paul, and Dorothy Zinberg. "Science and the Undergraduate." *Content and Context: Essays on College Education.* Ed. Carl Kaysen. New York: McGraw, 1973. 155–218.

Douglas, George H. "Business Writing in America in the Nineteenth Century." *Studies in the History of Business Writing.* Ed. George H. Douglas and Herbert W. Hildebrandt. Urbana: Association for Business Communication, 1985. 125–33.

Drewry, John E. "Journalistic Instruction in the South." *Journalism Quarterly* 4 (1927): 31–39.

DuBois, W. E. B. *Dusk of Dawn, an Essay Toward an Autobiography of a Race Concept.* New York: Harcourt, 1940.

Dyer, John P. *Tulane: The Biography of a University, 1834–1965.* New York: Harper, 1966.

Earle, Samuel C. "English in the Engineering School at Tufts College." *Proceedings of the Society for the Promotion of Engineering Education* 19 (1911): 33–47.

———. *The Theory and Practice of Technical Writing.* New York: Macmillan, 1911.

Eaton, Walter P. "Barrett Wendell." *American Mercury* 5 (1925): 448–55.

Eddy, Edward Danforth, Jr. *Colleges for Our Land and Time.* New York: Harper, 1956.

Edmonds, Walter D. Themes for English 12, 1924–25, ms. Pusey Library, Harvard U.

Emery, Edwin, and Michael Emery. *The Press and America: An Interpretive History of the Mass Media.* 4th ed. Englewood Cliffs: Prentice, 1978.

Esenwein, J. Berg, and Mary Eleanor Roberts. *The Art of Versification.* Springfield: Home Correspondence School, 1920.

Farrington, Frank. *Writing for the Trade Press.* Ridgewood, NJ: Editor, 1917.

Flint, L. N. "Comparing Notes on Journalism Courses." *Journalism Bulletin* 1 (1924): 84–85.

Forty-Eighth Annual Report of the President of Harvard College, 1872–1873. Cambridge: University Press, 1874.

Fountain, A. M. *A Study of Courses in Technical Writing.* State College Station Bulletin 15. Raleigh: North Carolina State College of Agriculture and Engineering, 1938.

Frankenburger, David B. "English at the University of Wisconsin." *English in American Universities.* Ed. William Morton Payne. Boston: Heath, 1910. 135–40.

Frederick, John T. "A Maker of Songs." *American Prefaces* 2 (March 1937): 83–84.

Freeman, John R. "A Plea for Breadth of Culture in the Technical School." *American Machinist* (12 Jan. 1905): 64.

Fullerton, W. M. Themes in English 5, Wendell, 1884–85, ms. Pusey Library, Harvard U.

Gardiner, J. H. Outline of English 12, 1898–99, ms. Pusey Library, Harvard U.

Garrett, George, ed. *Craft So Hard to Learn: Conversations with Poets and Novelists About the Teaching of Writing.* New York: Morrow, 1972.

Gaston, W. Themes for English 12, 1918–19, ms. Pusey Library, Harvard U.

Gaum, Carl G., and Harold F. Graves. *Report Writing.* New York: Prentice, 1929.

Gelb, Arthur, and Barbara Gelb. *O'Neill.* New York: Harper, 1973.

Gherardi, Bancroft, Jr. "The Proper Qualifications of Electrical Engineering School Graduates from the Telephone Engineer's Standpoint." *Transactions of the AIEE* 20 (1903): 579–86.

Given, John L. *Making a Newspaper.* New York: Holt, 1907.

Glaspell, Susan. *The Road to the Temple.* New York: Stokes, 1927.

Goodspeed, Thomas W. *A History of the University of Chicago.* 1916. Chicago: U of Chicago P, 1972.

Grabo, Carl H. *The Art of the Short Story.* New York: Scribner's, 1913.

"Guidelines and Directions for College Courses in Advanced Composition." *College Composition and Communication* 18 (1967): 266–68.

Guthrie, Warren. "Rhetorical Theory in Colonial America." *A History of Speech Education in America*. Ed. Karl R. Wallace. New York: Appleton, 1954. 48–59.

Handlin, Oscar, and Mary F. Handlin. *The American College and American Culture—Socialization as a Function of Higher Education*. New York: McGraw, 1970.

Haney's Guide to Authorship. New York: Haney, 1867.

Harbarger, Sara A. "Theme Subjects for Engineering Students." *English Journal* 5 (1916): 620–32.

Harrington, H. F., and T. T. Frankenberg. *Essentials in Journalism*. 1912. Rev. ed. Boston: Ginn, 1924.

Harvard Class of 1921: Twenty-First Anniversary Report. Cambridge: Harvard U, 1946.

Herrick, Robert. "Barrett Wendell." *New Republic* (10 Dec. 1924): 6–7.

Hill, Adams Sherman. "An Answer to the Cry for More English." *Good Company* 4 (1879): 233–40.

———. "English in Our Colleges." *Scribner's Magazine* 1 (January-June 1887): 507–12.

———. Lecture Notes from English 5, ms. Pusey Library, Harvard U.

———. *The Principles of Rhetoric and Their Application*. New York: Harper, 1878.

Historical Statistics of the United States: Colonial Times to 1970. Part 1. Washington: US Department of Commerce, Bureau of the Census, 1975.

Hofstadter, Richard. *The Age of Reform*. New York: Knopf, 1955.

Hotchkiss, George Burton, and Celia Anne Drew. *Business English: Its Principles and Practice*. New York: American Book, 1916.

Humphreys, Alexander. "Broader Training for the Engineer." *American Machinist* (29 Jan. 1903): 153–54.

Hyde, Grant Milnor. *Handbook for Newspaper Workers*. New York: Appleton, 1921.

———. "Raising the Quality of Students." *Journalism Bulletin* 4 (1927): 15–22.

Johnson, Burges. *Classes in "Journalistic Writing" and "Journalism."* Schenectady, NY: Union College, 1936.

————. *Creative Writing.* Syracuse: Syracuse U, 1934.

Johnson, Nan. *Nineteenth-Century Rhetoric in North America.* Carbondale: Southern Illinois UP, 1991.

"Journalism Education in the United States." *Journalism Bulletin* 3 (1926): 1–11.

Kinne, Wisner Payne. *George Pierce Baker and the American Theatre.* New York: Greenwood, 1968.

Kirby, Richard Shelton. *Inventors and Engineers of Old New Haven.* New Haven: New Haven Colony Historical Society, 1939.

Kitzhaber, Albert R. *Rhetoric in American Colleges, 1850–1900.* Dallas: Southern Methodist UP, 1990.

Klaw, Spencer. *The New Brahmins: Scientific Life in America.* New York: Morrow, 1968.

Lawless, Greg. *The Harvard Crimson Anthology: One Hundred Years at Harvard.* Boston: Houghton, 1980.

Lazell, Fred J. "Weeding Out the Unfit." *Journalism Bulletin* 4 (1927): 25–30.

Leaflets on English Courses, ts. Pusey Library, Harvard U.

Lee, James Melvin. *Instruction in Journalism in Institutions of Higher Education.* Department of the Interior Bureau of Education Bulletin 18. Washington: Government Printing Office, 1918.

LeVot, Andre. *F. Scott Fitzgerald: A Biography.* Trans. William Byron. New York: Doubleday, 1983.

Lewis, Edwin Herbert. *Business English.* 1911. Chicago: LaSalle Extension U, 1918.

Lyman, Rollo LaVerne. *English Grammar in American Schools Before 1850.* Washington: Government Printing Office, 1922.

Lyon, Leverett S. "The Business-English Situation in the Secondary Schools." *English Journal* 7 (1918): 576–87.

MacDougall, Curtis D. "Streamlining the Reporting Course." *Journalism Quarterly* 15 (1938): 282–88.

McGrath, Earl J. *Liberal Education in the Professions.* New York: Columbia U, 1959.

Maher, Stuart W., III. "The Origins of Technical Writing Instruction in the United States with a Survey of Technical

Writing Texts 1908–1977." M.A. Thesis. U of Tennessee, 1990.

Manchester, Frederick A. "Freshman English Once More?" *English Journal* 6 (1917): 295–307.

Mann, Charles Riborg. *A Study of Engineering Education.* Carnegie Foundation for the Advancement of Teaching, Bulletin 11. New York: Carnegie, 1918.

Mims, Edwin. *A History of Vanderbilt University.* Nashville: Vanderbilt UP, 1946.

Missions of the College Curriculum: A Contemporary Review with Suggestions. San Francisco: Jossey, 1977.

Morgan, Edmund S. *The Gentle Puritan.* New Haven: Yale UP, 1962.

Morison, Samuel Eliot. *The Development of Harvard University Since the Inauguration of President Eliot, 1869–1929.* Cambridge: Harvard UP, 1930.

Mott, Frank Luther. *American Journalism: A History, 1690–1960.* 3rd ed. New York: Macmillan, 1962.

———. *A History of American Magazines: 1885–1905.* Cambridge: Harvard UP, 1957.

Moxley, Joseph M. Introduction. *Creative Writing in America: Theory and Pedagogy.* Urbana: NCTE, 1989.

Munson, Gorham. *The Awakening Twenties.* Baton Rouge: Louisiana State UP, 1985.

Murphy, Lawrence W. "Professional and Nonprofessional Teaching of Journalism." *Journalism Quarterly* 9 (1932): 46–59.

Naether, Carl A., and George Francis Richardson. *A Course in English for Engineers.* 2 vols. Boston: Ginn, 1930.

Nash, Vernon. *Educating for Journalism.* New York: Columbia U, 1938.

Neal, Robert Wilson. *Short Stories in the Making.* New York: Oxford UP, 1914.

Nevins, Allan. *American Press Opinion: Washington to Coolidge.* Boston: Heath, 1928.

Nichols, Charles Washburn. "Teaching Shakespeare to Engineers." *English Journal* 2 (1913): 366–69.

"Notes of the Schools." *Journalism Bulletin* 1 (1924): 30–34.

O'Brien, Harry R. "Agricultural English." *English Journal* 3 (1914): 470–79.

O'Dell, De Forest. *The History of Journalism Education in the United States.* New York: Columbia U Teachers College Bureau of Publications, 1935.

O'Neill, Eugene. "Professor G. P. Baker." *New York Times* (13 Jan. 1935), sec. 9, i.

Osgood, Charles G. "No Set Requirement of English Composition in the Freshman Year." *English Journal* 4 (1915): 231–35.

Park, Clyde W. *English Applied in Technical Writing.* New York: Crofts, 1926.

Parsons, James Russell. "Professional Education." *Monographs on Education in the United States.* Vol. 2. Ed. Nicholas Murray Butler. Albany: Lyon, 1900. 467–549.

Peterson, Paul V. "1984 Survey: No Change in Mass Comm Enrollments." *Journalism Educator* 40.1 (1985): 3–9.

Popham, Donald F. *Foundations of Secondary Education: Historical, Comparative, and Curricular.* Minneapolis: Burgess, 1969.

Potter, W. J. Themes and Forensics, 1854, ms. Pusey Library, Harvard U.

Pulitzer, Joseph. "The Columbia Agreement and the Will: Two Key Documents of 1903/04." *Education in Journalism.* Ed. Heinz-Dietrich Fischer and Christopher G. Trump. Bochum, West Germany: Studienverlag, 1980. 11–17.

———. "Planning a School of Journalism—The Basic Concept in 1904." *Education in Journalism.* Ed. Heinz-Dietrich Fischer and Christopher G. Trump. Bochum, West Germany: Studienverlag, 1980. 18–60.

Ralph, Julian. *The Making of a Journalist.* New York: Harper, 1903.

Ranlett, Louis F. English 5, Themes, 1920–21, ms. Pusey Library, Harvard U.

Reid, Whitelaw. "Journalism as a Career." *American and English Studies.* Vol. 2. 1913. Freeport: Books for Libraries, 1968. 193–227.

Report of the Committee of Ten on Secondary School Studies, with the Reports of the Conferences Arranged by the Committee. New York: American, 1894.

"The Report of the Committee on Schools of Journalism to the A.S.N.E." *Journalism Quarterly* 7 (1930): 142–53.

Report to the Corporation of Brown University. Providence: Whitney, 1850.

Rickard, T. A. *A Guide to Technical Writing.* San Francisco: Mining and Scientific Press, 1908.

———. *Retrospect: An Autobiography.* New York: McGraw, 1937.

Robbins, Harry Wolcott, and Roscoe Edward Parker. *Advanced Exposition.* 1933. New York: Prentice, 1935.

Root, Charles T. "The History and Development of Industrial Journalism." *Lectures in the Forum in Industrial Journalism.* Ed. Albert Frederick Wilson. New York: Advertising and Selling, 1915.

Ross, Earle D. *Democracy's College: The Land-Grant Movement in the Formative Stage.* Ames, Iowa: Iowa State College P, 1942.

Rudolph, Frederick. *The American College and University.* New York: Knopf, 1962.

———. *Curriculum: A History of the American Undergraduate Course of Study Since 1636.* San Francisco: Jossey, 1977.

Rudy, Willis. *The Evolving Liberal Arts Curriculum: A Historical Review of Basic Themes.* New York: Teachers College, Columbia U, 1960.

Russell, David R. *Writing in the Academic Disciplines, 1870–1990: A Curricular History.* Carbondale: Southern Illinois UP, 1991.

Scott, Fred Newton. "English Composition as a Mode of Behavior." *English Journal* 11 (1922): 463–73.

———. "The Standard of American Speech." *English Journal* 6 (1917): 1–11.

Scott, Fred N., George R. Carpenter, and Franklin T. Baker. *The Teaching of English in the Elementary and the Secondary School.* New York: Longmans, 1903.

Scott, Fred N., and Joseph V. Denney. *Paragraph-Writing.* Ann Arbor: Register, 1891.

Scudder, Horace E. *Literature in School, an Address and Two Essays.* Boston: Houghton, 1888.

See, Horace. "President's Address, 1888." *Transactions of the American Society of Mechanical Engineers* 10 (1888–89): 482–98.

Self, Robert T. *Barrett Wendell.* Boston: Twayne, 1975.

Shelnutt, Eve. "Notes from a Cell: Creative Writing Programs in Isolation." *Creative Writing in America: Theory and Pedagogy.* Ed. Joseph M. Moxley. Urbana: NCTE, 1989. 25–45.

Shuman, Edwin L. *Practical Journalism.* New York: Appleton, 1903.

Simmons, John O. "The Non-Professional Student in Journalism." *Journalism Bulletin* 3 (1926): 32–37.

Slosson, Edwin E. *Great American Universities.* New York: Macmillan, 1910.

Smart, Walter Kay. *How to Write Business Letters.* Chicago: Shaw, 1916.

Smith, Oberlin. "President's Annual Address: The Engineer as a Scholar and a Gentleman." *Transactions of the American Society of Mechanical Engineers* 12 (1890–91): 42–55.

Spencer, M. Lyle. *Editorial Writing: Ethics, Policy, Practice.* Boston: Houghton, 1924.

———. *News Writing: The Gathering and Handling of News Stories.* New York: Heath, 1917.

Stegner, Wallace. Introduction. *Twenty Years of Stanford Short Stories.* Ed. Wallace Stegner and Richard Scowcroft. Stanford: Stanford UP, 1966. ix–xx.

Steinmetz, Charles P. "Presidential Address." *Transactions of the AIEE* 19 (1902): 1145–50.

Stevens, Robert. *Law School: Legal Education in America from the 1850s to the 1980s.* Chapel Hill: U of North Carolina P, 1983.

Stewart, Donald C. "The Barnyard Goose, History, and Fred Newton Scott." *English Journal* 67 (1978): 14–17.

———. "Rediscovering Fred Newton Scott." *College English* 40 (1979): 539–47.

Storey, Charles M. Composition for English 12, 1911, ms. Pusey Library, Harvard U.

Strange, W. W. Letter to the Editor. *Mining and Scientific Press* 99 (1909): 668.

Strauss, Louis A. "Regents Merge Two Departments." *Michigan Alumnus* 36 (1930): 331–332+.

Sutton, Albert. *Education for Journalism in the United States from Its Beginning to 1940.* Northwestern University Studies in the Humanities 10. Evanston: Northwestern U, 1945.

Swan, C. J. Themes for English 18, 1889-90, ms. Pusey Library, Harvard U.

Sypherd, W. O., and Sharon Brown. *The Engineer's Manual of English.* Chicago: Scott, 1933.

Teaching Creative Writing. Washington: Library of Congress, 1974.

Tebbel, John. *A History of Book Publishing in the United States.* Vol. 2. New York: Bowker, 1975.

Thompson, Lawrance. *Robert Frost, the Early Years, 1874–1915.* New York: Holt, 1966.

Thompson, Lawrance, and R. H. Winnick. *Robert Frost: A Biography.* New York: Holt, 1981.

Thorne, Barrie. "Professional Education in Law." *Education for the Professions of Medicine, Law, Theology, and Social Welfare.* Ed. Everett C. Hughes et al. New York: McGraw, 1973.

Thorpe, Clarence D. "The Department of Rhetoric." *The University of Michigan: An Encyclopedic Survey.* Vol. 2. Ed. Wilfred R. Shaw. Ann Arbor: U of Michigan P, 1951.

Thurber, Edward A. "Composition in Our Colleges." *English Journal* 4 (1915): 9–14.

Thwing, Charles F. *A History of Higher Education in America.* New York: Appleton, 1906.

Turnbull, Andrew, ed. *The Letters of F. Scott Fitzgerald.* New York: Scribner's, 1963.

Turneaure, F. E. "The Engineering School in the United States." *Wisconsin Engineering* 9 (June 1905): 274–75.

Twenty Years of School and College English. Cambridge: Harvard U, 1896.

"The Undergraduate Advanced Composition Course." *College Composition and Communication* 14 (1963): 190.

Veysey, Laurence. "Stability and Experiment in the American Undergraduate Curriculum." *Content and Context: Essays on College Education.* Ed. Carl Kaysen. New York: McGraw, 1973. 1–63.

Walker, Franklin. *Frank Norris, a Biography.* New York: Doubleday, 1932.

Wallace, Una. "A Singing Professor." *Daily Iowan* (6 December 1931), Sunday Magazine Section: 1+.

Watt, Homer Andrew. *The Composition of Technical Papers.* New York: McGraw, 1917.

Webster, Edward Harlan. "Preparation in English for Business." *English Journal* 1 (1912): 613–17.

Weeks, Francis W. "The Teaching of Business Writing at the Collegiate Level 1900–1920." *Studies in the History of Business Writing.* Ed. George H. Douglas and Herbert W. Hildebrandt. Urbana: Association for Business Communication, 1985. 201–15.

Wendell, Barrett. "English at Harvard." *Dial* 26 (1894): 131–33.

———. *English Composition.* New York: Scribner's, 1891.

———. *A Literary History of America.* 1904. New York: Scribner's, 1928.

———. Notes for English A, 1889–90, ms. Pusey Library, Harvard U.

———. Notes of Lectures in English 12, 1885–87, ms. Pusey Library, Harvard U.

———. "Of Education." *The Privileged Classes.* New York: Scribner's, 1908. 181–274.

———. "The Study of Expression." *The Mystery of Education and Other Academic Performances.* New York: Scribner's, 1909. 137–194.

Wendell, Barrett, and Chester Noyes Greenough. *A History of Literature in America.* New York: Scribner's, 1904.

Westlake, J. Willis. *How to Write Letters: A Manual of Correspondence.* Philadelphia: Sower, 1876.

White, Andrew D. "The Need of Another University." *Forum* 6 (1889): 465–73.

White, J. G. "The Problems That Are Facing the Electrical Engineer of To-day and the Qualities of Mind and Character Which Are Needed to Meet Them." *Transactions of the AIEE* 20 (1903): 569–78.

Wilbers, Stephen. *The Iowa Writers' Workshop: Origins, Emergence, and Growth.* Iowa City: U of Iowa P, 1980.

Wiley, H. W. "The Role of Chemistry in University Education." *Science* 16 (1902): 842–50.

Will, Allen Sinclair. "Concerning the Status of Teachers." *Journalism Quarterly* 5 (1928): 18–19.

———. *Education for Newspaper Life.* Newark: Essex, 1931.

Williams, Sara L. *Twenty Years of Education for Journalism.* Columbia, MO: Stephens, 1929.

Williams, Walter, and Frank L. Martin. *The Practice of Journalism.* Columbia, MO: Missouri Book, 1911.

Wilmer, Lambert A. *Our Press Gang.* Philadelphia: Lloyd, 1859.

Wilson, Albert Frederick. Introduction. *Lectures in the Forum in Industrial Journalism.* New York: Advertising and Selling, 1915.

Wilson, Logan, and Charles G. Dobbins. "Colleges and Universities." *Encyclopedia Americana.* 1990 ed.

Wingate, Charles F. *Views and Interviews on Journalism.* New York: Patterson, 1875.

Winterowd, W. Ross. "Transferable and Local Writing Skills." *Journal of Advanced Composition* 1 (Spring 1980): 1–3.

Witt, Peter D. The Beginnings of the Teaching of the Vernacular Literature in the Secondary Schools of Massachusetts. Diss. Harvard U, 1968. Ann Arbor: UMI, 1982. 6911507.

Witte, Stephen P. *A National Survey of College and University Writing Program Directors.* Writing Program Assessment Project. Austin: U of Texas, 1983. ED 210709.

Wolfe, Thomas. *Of Time and the River.* New York: Scribner's, 1935.

Woolley, Edwin C. *New Handbook of Composition.* 1907. Boston: Heath, 1926.

Wozniak, John Michael. *English Composition in Eastern Colleges, 1850–1940.* Washington, DC: UP of America, 1978.

Index

Abbott, Edwin. Work: *How to Write Clearly,* 19
Adams, Francis, 20
Adams, John Quincy, 31
Addison, Joseph, 67
Advanced Exposition (Robbins and Parker), 58
advanced writing courses: academic security of, 148; collegial atmosphere of, 41–42; common history of, ix, x, xi, 147; as corrective for deficiencies in curriculum, 36–37; criticisms of, ix; daily themes in, 37–38, 40–41, 48–51, 54, 55; demand for, 23, 26, 35; eclectic approach to, 151–54; as elective, 12, 37, 58, 59–60; encouragement of individuality in, 37–38, 47–48, 56; as extension of freshman composition, 57, 58; forensic exercises in, 40; generalized approach in, 37–55, 60, 61, 62, 63–64; growth of, 148, 149–50; individual conferences in, 41, 45; limited creative opportunities in, 72; practical emphasis in, 148, 151; as preparation for professions, 43–44, 46, 52–53, 56, 61–62; as requirement, 12, 58, 59; rhetorical influence in, 150; search for common

definition of, 58–59; segmentation of, ix–x, x–xi, 61–69, 147; selection of textbooks for, 58; spread of, from Harvard, 55–57; study of argumentation in, 53–54; style as subject of, 41–42, 46, 49–51; theme topics for, 37–38, 38–39; validity of, 150; workshop setting of, 38, 40, 41, 44–45, 52, 54–55, 56–57, 63–64; writing from literary models in, 43. *See also* business writing courses; creative writing courses; journalism courses; technical writing courses
Agg, Thomas. Work: *The Preparation of Engineering Reports,* 139
agricultural English courses, 140
agricultural journalism, 131–33, 140
Agricultural Journalism (Crawford and Rogers), 132
agriculture, demand for competent writing, 123, 128–29
agriculture programs: degree of specialized training in, 124; enrollment of students in journalism classes, 130; growth of, 123–24; introduction into universities, 125, 126; professional support for, 127
Alabama Polytechnic Institute, 133

Altmaier, Carl Lewis. Works:
  Commercial Correspondence,
  143; *Postal Information*, 143
Alworthy, Hollis (*Harvard
  Lampoon* character), 42–43
American Association of
  Newspaper Editors, 101–2
American Association of Schools
  and Departments of
  Journalism, 104, 116
American Association of Teachers
  in Journalism, 116
American Bicycling Journal, 14
American Engineer (journal), 133
American Institute of Electrical
  Engineers, 128
The American Legion Weekly, 46
American Society of Mechanical
  Engineers (ASME), 28–29
Amherst College, 55, 93
Anderson, Sherwood, 91
*Annual Reports of Harvard
  College*, 19–20, 21
Ansley, Clarke Fisher, 87, 91
anti-intellectualism: in creative
  writing, 97; in journalism,
  116
Applebee, Arthur N., 17, 18, 21
apprenticeships: college courses as,
  151; professional training
  through, 1, 5; training of
  printers through, 99–100
Archer, William. Work: *Play
  Making: A Manual of
  Craftsmanship*, 77
Argosy magazine, 71
argument: advanced study of,
  53–54, 55–56, 57, 62, 63,
  67, 69; instruction on, in
  required composition courses,
  12, 23; and journalistic
  writing, 107. *See also*
  disputations (forensics)
Argus of Western America
  (newspaper), 31
Aristotle, 2. Work: *Poetics*, 80

Arizona State University, 153
Arnold, Matthew, 17, 69, 135.
  Work: *Culture and Anarchy*,
  17
Arthur, Chester A., 39
The Art of the Short Story (Grabo),
  74, 76
Asker, William, 25
Associated Press, 101, 114, 117,
  118
ateliers libres (informal academies),
  52
Atkinson, W. P., 27
Atlanta Constitution (newspaper),
  109
Atlantic Monthly, 39
audience analysis: by business
  writing students, 143–44;
  by journalists, 108–9; by
  technical writers, 138–39,
  150, 151
Austen, Jane, 38
Aydelotte, Frank, 69, 134–35.
  Work: *English and
  Engineering*, 135

Bain, Alexander. Work: *English
  Composition and Rhetoric*, 12
Baker, Franklin T., 24
Baker, George Pierce, 90, 93;
  composition classes of,
  53–54; creative writing
  courses of, 79–86;
  justification of creative
  writing curriculum, 78. Work:
  Dramatic Technique, 77, 78
Baker, Harry T., 53, 94–95
Baker, Roy P. Work: *The
  Preparation of Reports:
  Engineering, Scientific,
  Administrative*, 138, 140
"Barbara on the Beach" (Millay),
  74
Barbed Wire (Piper), 87
Barbed Wire and Wayfarers
  (Piper), 87

Barnard College, 74
Barrett, Charles Raymond, 88–89.
    Work: *Short Story Writing,* 74
Bates, Arlo, 52
Baton Rouge States-Times, 117–18
Battle, Kemp P., 9–10
Bennett, James Gordon, 32, 33
Berkeley, Frances. Work: *A College
    Course in Writing from
    Models,* 57
Bernstein, Carl, 149
Bessie Tift College, 103
Bicycling World (magazine), 14
Bigelow, Marshall. Work:
    Handbook of Punctuation, 12
Bishop, John Peale, 89–90
blacks, and land grant colleges, 8
Blaine, James, 42
Blair, Hugh, 4. Work: *Lectures on
    Rhetoric and Belles Lettres,* 4,
    17
Bledstein, Burton J., 6, 14, 46
Bleyer, Willard, 67–68. Works:
    *How to Write Special Feature
    Articles,* 68; *Newspaper
    Writing and Editing,* 68;
    Types of News Writing, 68,
    106, 107
book publishing: and creation of
    demand for writers, 14–15;
    employment of writers in, 90
Bortin, Ruth V., 88
Bound East for Cardiff (O'Neill),
    80, 90
Bowdoin College, 56
Braddock, Richard, 59
Bread Loaf Writers' Conference,
    82, 96
Brewster, William T., 74
Briggs, LeBaron Russell,
    composition courses of,
    43–46, 47–48, 52, 53, 55, 57
Brittin, Norman A., 74
Brooks, Van Wyck, 89
Broome, Edwin C., 18
Broun, Heywood, 82–83, 86

Brown, Alice, 71
Brown, John Mason, 82
Brown, Rollo, 44–45, 47–48
Brown, Sharon. Work: *The
    Engineer's Manual of English,*
    138
Browne, Michael Denis, 94
Brown University, 10–11
Bryant, William Cullen, 89
Buck, Gertrude, 25–26
Burdett, Cyril Herbert, 50
Burke, Edmund, 38
Burke, Kenneth, 90
business: administration of,
    126–27; demand for
    competent writing, 15, 26,
    35, 123, 146; etiquette
    manuals for, 142
Business English (E. Lewis),
    135–36
*Business English: Principles and
    Practice* (Hotchkiss and
    Drew), 143
business programs: degree of
    specialized training in, 124;
    growth of, 123–24, 145; in
    high schools, 127;
    introduction into universities,
    126, 127
business writing courses: academic
    security of, 145–46, 148;
    attention to form, 142–45,
    148; attention to style, 143;
    business professionals as
    teachers of, 141–42; demand
    for, 129; for engineers,
    135–36; growth of, 144, 145,
    149, 150; instruction in
    audience analysis, 143–44;
    introduction of, 62, 63, 66,
    68, 69, 70, 124–25, 140–41;
    journalistic approach in, 130,
    133–34; practical emphasis in,
    148; status as specialty, 146;
    textbooks for, 142–44; types
    of, 129–30

Butts, R. Freeman, 2
Byron, George Gordon, Lord, 39

Cabell, James Branch, 71
Cable, George Washington, 88, 89
Cairns, William B., 67. Works:
    The Forms of Discourse, 67;
    Introduction to Rhetoric, 67
California State University,
    Fullerton, 153
Calvert, Monte A., 28
Cambridge High School, 18
Camp, Eugene M., 100–101,
    102
Campbell, George, 22. Work:
    Philosophy of Rhetoric, 4
Campbell, John, 31
Capen, Samuel P., 7
Carhart, Henry, 30
Carlyle, Thomas, 135
Carnegie University, 136
Carpenter, George R., 24, 26, 58.
    Work: *Exercises in Rhetoric
    and English Composition*, 12
Carruth, William Herbert, 72,
    78–79. Work: *Verse Writing*,
    72, 75
Cather, Willa, 71
Century magazine, 71
*Century Readings for a Course in
    English Literature* (Young),
    68
Chaucer, Geoffrey, 10, 11, 69
Cheit, Earl F., 27–28, 123, 125
Chicago Evening Post, 87
Chicago Herald, 109
Chicago Record-Herald, 105
Chicago Tribune, 100, 104, 109
Christensen, Francis, 59
The Christian Endeavor World
    (magazine), 46
Cicero. Work: *De Oratore*, 4
civil service, creation of demand
    for competent writing, 15
Civil War, 17, 40, 126, 142
Clark, Thomas Arkle, 140

classical curriculum: influence of
    scientific method on, 3–4;
    irrelevance to industrial
    society, 6; lecture and
    recitation method in, 2–3; in
    primary schools, 16–17;
    replacement by specialized
    training, 6–10, 15
Cleveland, Grover, 42
Clyde, Thomas, 49
coherence, as principle of
    composition, 13, 23, 24
Cole, Richard R., 121
Colgate College, 55
*A College Course in Writing from
    Models* (Berkeley), 57
College Minerva (newspaper), 112
College of New Jersey, 18. *See also*
    Princeton University
College of Pennsylvania, 2, 5
Collier's magazine, 71
Columbia University, 103;
    advanced writing courses at,
    55; enrollment figures, 5;
    journalism instruction at,
    103–4, 130; technical
    programs at, 125
Commercial Correspondence
    (Altmaier), 143
Commission on the Secondary
    School Curriculum, 73
composition: courses for teachers
    of, 64; entrance-level
    proficiency for colleges,
    18–20
composition courses: primary and
    secondary, college
    recommendations concerning,
    21–22; in professionalized
    curriculum, 11–14; in
    training of engineers, 27, 28.
    See also advanced writing
    courses; business writing
    courses; creative writing
    courses; freshman
    composition courses;

journalism courses; technical
writing courses

*The Composition of Technical
Papers* (Watt), 137–38

Conference on College Composition and Communication
(CCCC), 58–59

conferences, student-teacher, 41,
45, 80

Connors, Robert, ix, 22, 27, 29,
139, 145, 149

Conrad, Lawrence H., 73

Cook, George Cram (Jig), 86–87,
90, 91

Cooper, James Fenimore, 32–33.
Works: *Home as Found*, 33;
Homeward Bound, 32–33

Copeland, Charles Townsend, 11,
20, 52–53, 55, 57

Cornell University, 6–7, 8–9, 100

correspondence, business, 142–45

Counts, George S., 21

A Course in English for Engineers
(Naether and Richardson),
136

A Course in Journalistic Writing
(Hyde), 68

Cowan, Louise, 91–92, 94

Cowley, Malcolm, 90, 91

Cowper, William, 11

Crane, Stephen, 91

Crawford, Nelson Antrim. Work:
Agricultural Journalism, 132

creative writing: in generalized
composition courses, 70;
inspiration in, 77–78;
rebellion against academia,
89–93; return to campus,
93–98

creative writing courses: academic
security of, 148; attention to
form in, 74–75, 77, 147;
attention to planning, 75–77;
attention to technique, 81,
82; benefits of, 70;
contradictory goals of, 73;

and demand for writers,
71–72; encouragement of, by
specialized curriculum, 70,
72; excesses of student
writers, 82–85; growth of,
98, 149; individual
conferences in, 80; influence
of, 81; introduction of, 62,
63, 64, 66, 69, 70–71,
73–74; problems of, 96–97,
98; professional writers as
instructors of, 93–94, 96–97,
98, 149; and progressive
education movement, 72–73;
study of literature in, 66, 74,
77, 78, 88–89, 151;
textbooks for, 74–78; validity
of, 62, 73; workshop setting
of, 78–89, 93–97, 148, 151

Creek, Herbert L., 139, 141–42

criticism, advanced study of,
64, 66

Culture and Anarchy (Arnold), 17

cummings, e. e., 90

Cunliffe, John William, 103–4

Daily Iowan, 118

daily themes, 37–38, 40–41,
48–51, 54, 55

Daley, John M., 112

Darrow, Clarence, 91

Dartmouth, Lord, 31

Dartmouth College, 5, 55, 56

Dartmouth Gazette, 112

Davidson, Donald, 91, 92–93,
94, 96

de Billier, William Bayard, 51

democracy, and literary education,
17

Demosthenes, 6

Denney, Joseph, 58. Work:
Paragraph-Writing, 24

Denton, L. W., 142

Denver University, 100

De Oratore (Cicero), 4

DePaul University, 144

DeQuincey, Thomas, 67
description: instruction on, in
    required composition courses,
    12; and journalistic writing,
    107; study of, in advanced
    writing courses, 51, 57, 63,
    67, 68; technical, 137
Des Moines Register, 118
Dewey, John, 72–73. Work: "The
    Ethics of Democracy," 72–73
Digest of Educational Statistics,
    123–24
discourse: advanced study of, 63,
    67, 68; exercises in, 25;
    instruction on, in required
    composition courses, 12, 13,
    23, 24; irrelevance of forms
    of, to journalistic writing,
    107, 108; rules of, as
    restriction on creativity, 72;
    study of forms by technical
    writers, 137, 138, 139
disputations (forensics): in
    advanced writing courses, 40;
    on current issues, 3–4, 5;
    syllogistic, 3. *See also*
    argument
Dobbins, Charles G., 5
Dos Passos, John, 90
Douglas, George H., 126–27
Doyle, Arthur Conan, 88–89
drama (plays): birth of modern era
    of, 81; excesses of student
    writers, 82–85; experimental,
    off-campus performance of,
    90; form in, 77; planning of,
    77; student, staging of,
    85–86; technique in, 81, 82;
    workshops in, 79–86, 95, 96
Dramatic Technique (G. P. Baker),
    77, 78
Dreiser, Theodore, 91
Drew, Celia Ann. Work: *Business
    English: Principles and
    Practice,* 143
Drewry, John E., 131, 133

Drexel Institute, 133
Dryden, John, 11
Dry Goods Economist (journal),
    133
DuBois, W. E. B., 47
The Duchess Emilia (Wendell),
    42, 43
Dugard, William, 3
du Pont, Henry, 126
Duruy, Victor. Work: *Histoire des
    Temps Modernes,* 27
Dutton, E. P., 14
Dyer, John P., 112

E. I. du Pont de Nemours and
    Co., 126
Earle, Samuel Chandler, 138.
    Work: *The Theory and Practice
    of Technical Writing,* 137
Eaton, Walter P., 42, 47
Eddy, Edward Danforth, 7, 8, 10,
    27, 125, 126, 127–28
Edgeworth, Maria, 38
editorial writing: audience for,
    108–9; as craft, 105–6; form
    in, 107; practical experience
    in, 115, 117, 118
Editorial Writing (Spencer),
    105–6, 107, 108–9
Edmonds, Walter D., 53
Effective Business Letters
    (Gardner), 68, 143
elective system: advanced
    composition in, 12, 37, 58,
    59–60; and composition
    requirement, 11–12; English
    courses available under, 11;
    establishment and expansion
    of, 7, 10; and requirements of
    professional education, 8–9, 10
elementary schools. *See* primary
    schools
Elements of Rhetoric (Whately), 4
Eliot, Charles, 7, 19, 21
Eliot, George, 13
Eliot, T. S., 90, 93

Elliott, William, 91–92
Emerson, Ralph Waldo, 6, 135
Emery, Edwin, 31
Emery, Michael, 31
engineering: deficiencies of
    writing in, 27, 29–30;
    demand for competent
    writing, 123
Engineering and Mining Journal,
    136
engineering English courses,
    27–28, 28–29, 134–40
engineering journalism, 131, 132,
    133
engineering programs: business
    emphasis in, 135–36; degree
    of specialized training in,
    124; enrollment of students
    in journalism classes, 130;
    growth of, 123–24, 145;
    humanistic training in,
    27–28, 28–29, 65, 68–69,
    127–28, 134–35;
    introduction into universities,
    125, 126; specialized training
    in, 28, 128
The Engineering Record (journal),
    29
The Engineer's Manual of English
    (Sypherd and Brown), 138
*The Engineer's Professional and
    Business Writing* (Naether and
    Richardson), 136
Engle, Paul, 71, 96
English and Engineering
    (Aydelotte), 135
*English Applied in Technical
    Writing* (Park), 138–39
English Composition (Wendell), 12,
    23, 55
English Composition and Rhetoric
    (Bain), 12
English courses: for agriculture
    students, 140; impact of
    professionalized curriculum
    on, 10–14; in primary and

secondary schools, 17–18; in
    primary and secondary
    schools—inadequacy of,
    19–21, 34–35; in primary and
    secondary schools—reforms to
    suit colleges, 21–22; in
    training of engineers, 27–28,
    28–29, 134–40. *See also*
    advanced writing courses;
    business writing courses;
    composition courses; creative
    writing courses; freshman
    composition courses;
    journalism courses; technical
    writing courses
English departments: dissociation
    of journalism from, 116, 120,
    121; eclectic writing
    programs in, 152–54;
    relationship of specialized
    writing courses to, 148;
    separation of business and
    technical writing instructors
    from, 146; separation of
    creative writing instructors
    from, 96, 97; technical and
    business writing in, 124,
    129–30, 134–46
English for Engineers (Harbarger),
    140
English Grammar (Lowth), 4
English Journal, 24–25
English language: in classical
    education, 3; and increasing
    practicality of education, 3, 4
English Language (Lounsbury), 11
entrance examinations, 18–19,
    20, 22
Errors in the Use of English
    (Hodgson), 12
Esenwein, J. Berg, 78. Work:
    Writing the Short-Story,
    75–76
"Essay on Comedy" (Meredith),
    80
Essay on Liberty (J. S. Mill), 41

Essays for College Men: Education, Science, and Art (Young), 68
Essentials in Journalism (Harrington and Frankenberg), 109
"The Ethics of Democracy," (Dewey), 72–73
Evangeline (Longfellow), 21
Exercises in English (Woolley), 67
Exercises in Rhetoric and English Composition (Carpenter), 12
exposition: instruction on, in required composition courses, 12, 23; and journalistic writing, 107; study of, in advanced writing courses, 54, 57, 58, 63, 67, 68, 69; technical, 137

faculty psychology, emphasis on recitation, 3
Farrington, Frank. Work: *Writing for the Trade Press*, 133–34
fiction, publication in magazines, 71–72. *See also* short story
First Bunker Hill Oration, 21
Fitzgerald, F. Scott, 89–90. Work: *This Side of Paradise*, 90
Flint, L. N., 116
Flint, Seth, 83–85
Florida State College of Agriculture, 27
Fordham College, 73
forensics. *See* disputations (forensics)
forestry programs: enrollment of students in journalism classes, 130; growth of, 123–24
form, study of: by business writing students, 142–45, 148; by creative writers, 74–75, 77, 147; by journalism students, 107–8, 109, 111–12, 119, 121, 147–48; by technical writing students, 132, 136, 137, 138, 139, 145, 148, 151

The Forms of Discourse (Cairns), 67
47 Workshop, 85–86
Forum in Industrial Journalism, 133
Foster, Walter. Work: *The Preparation of Engineering Reports*, 139
Foundations of Rhetoric (Hill), 40
Fountain, A. M., 133, 136, 139–40
Frankenberg, Theodore. Work: *Essentials in Journalism*, 109
Frankenburger, David B., 67
Frederick, John, 88, 91, 95
Freeman, John R., 28–29
freshman composition courses: content of, 12, 22; limitations of, 22–26, 35, 36, 72; preoccupation with grammar, 110–11; as requirement, 36, 37; rhetorical influence in, 150; technical students in, 139, 140
Freshman English: A Manual (Young), 68
Frost, Robert, 47, 91, 93–94
The Fugitive (journal), 92
Fullerton, William Morton, 41, 42

Gardiner, John, 52, 55
Gardner, Edward Hall, 68, 141. Work: *Effective Business Letters*, 68, 143
Gardner Lyceum, 125
Garrett, George, 94, 96–97
Gaston, William, 52
Gates, Lewis Edwards, 54–55
Gaum, Carl G., 137. Work: *Report Writing*, 138, 139
Gazette (Tulane College newspaper), 112
Gelb, Arthur, 79–80, 86
Gelb, Barbara, 79–80, 86
Genung, John Franklin, 58

Georgetown University, 112
German language, study by
    engineers, 27–28
German university system, 6–7
Gherardi, Bancroft, 128
Given, John L. Work: *Making a
    Newspaper,* 105
Glaspell, Susan, 71, 86, 87
Godkin, E. L., 14, 20
Goldsmith, Oliver, 52. Work: *The
    Vicar of Wakefield,* 19
Goodspeed, Thomas W., 112
Goss, William F. M., 28
Goucher College, 94–95
Grabo, Carl H. Work: *The Art of
    the Short Story,* 74, 76
grammar: in development of
    composition skill, 22, 25–26;
    entrance-level proficiency for
    colleges, 18–20;
    preoccupation of freshman
    composition with, 110–11;
    primary and secondary
    instruction in, 17; primary
    and secondary instruction
    in—college recommendations
    concerning, 21; relationship
    to meaning, 25–26; rules
    of, as restriction on creativity,
    72; study by technical writing
    students, 137, 138, 139
Graves, Harold F., 137. Work:
    Report Writing, 138, 139
Great Britain, composition courses
    in, 62
Great Depression, 148
Greek language, in classical
    education, 2, 3
Greeley, Horace, 40, 100, 132
A Guide to Technical Writing
    (Rickard), 136–37
Guild, Thacher Howland, 140–41
Guizot, François. Work: *History of
    Civilization in Europe,* 27
Gurney, E. W., 19–20
Guthrie, Warren, 3

Haldeman, Samuel S. Work:
    Outlines of Etymology, 11
Hamilton, Alexander, 31
Hamilton College, 55, 56, 62, 63
Hamlet (Shakespeare), 21
Hammett, Dashiell, 90
Hammond reports, 124
Handbook for Newspaper Workers
    (Hyde), 68, 110–11
Handbook of Composition
    (Woolley), 67, 110–11
Handbook of Punctuation
    (Bigelow), 12
Handlin, Mary F., 6
Handlin, Oscar, 6
Haney's Guide to Authorship, 104
Harbarger, Sara. Work: *English for
    Engineers,* 140
Harper's Magazine, 39
Harrington, Harry. Work:
    Essentials in Journalism, 109
Harris, Joel Chandler, 88
Harte, Bret, 88, 89
Harvard Class of 1921, 46
Harvard College: classical
    curriculum at, 2; creative
    writing courses at, 73, 79–86,
    93; enrollment figures, 5;
    entrance exams at, 18–20, 22;
    generalized approach to
    advanced composition at,
    37–55, 61, 74, 86; impact of
    professionalization on English
    courses, 11–13; limitations of
    freshman composition at,
    23–24; medical school
    admissions requirements, 5;
    professionalization of
    curriculum of, 6, 7;
    proficiency of entering
    freshman at, 19–21, 22;
    revision of classical
    curriculum at, 4–5; student
    newspapers at, 112–14;
    student themes about, 38–39,
    51–52

Harvard Crimson (newspaper), 112–14
Harvard Lampoon, 42–43
Harvard Magenta (newspaper), 112
Harvard Monthly, 47
Hawthorne, Nathaniel, 74, 88, 89
Hearn, Lafcadio, 89
Hebrew language, in classical education, 2, 3
Hedge, Levi. Work: *Logick,* 4
Hemingway, Ernest, 90, 91
Henry, O., 71
Herald (newspaper), 31
Herrick, Robert, 47, 55–56, 66
higher education: adoption of entrance exams, 18–19, 20, 22; changes in primary and secondary English mandated by, 21–22; classical curriculum in, 2–3; dissatisfaction with primary and secondary English, 19–21, 35; entry of technical fields into, 125–30; introduction of practicality into, 3–6; as preparation for journalists, 99–103; professionalization of, 6–10; as professional training, 1; progressive philosophy in, 73; rebellion of creative writers against, 89–93; in reform of journalism, 34, 106; return of creative writers to, 93–98
high schools. *See* secondary schools
Hill, A. S., 11, 43, 58; on class criticism of themes, 38; composition courses of, 37–40, 55, 57; on forensic exercises, 40; on limitations of freshman composition course, 23; on neglect of quality writing, 36; on primary and secondary English education, 19, 20;

professional background of, 39–40; recognition of need for creative writing, 72; on theme topics, 37–38. Works: *Foundations of Rhetoric,* 40; *Principles of Rhetoric,* 12, 22–23, 38, 39, 40
Hirsch, Nat, 91, 92
Hirsch, Sidney, 91, 92
Histoire des Temps Modernes (Duruy), 27
Historical Statistics of the United States, 15
History of Civilization in Europe (Guizot), 27
History of English Literature (Taine), 11
Hobart College, 10–11
Hobbes, Thomas. Work: *The Leviathan,* 50
Hodgson, William B. Work: *Errors in the Use of English,* 12
Hollins College, 96
Holmes, Oliver Wendell, 51, 89
Holt, Henry, 14
Home as Found (Cooper), 33
Homer, 6, 38
Homeward Bound (Cooper), 32–33
Hopkins, Edwin M., 103, 111, 114–15
Horace, 6
Hotchkiss, George Burton, 141. Work: *Business English: Principles and Practice,* 143
Houp, Kenneth W. Work: *Reporting Technical Information,* 145
Housman, A. E., 71
Howells, William Dean, 88
How to Write Business Letters (Smart), 143–44
How to Write Clearly (Abbott), 19
How to Write Letters: A Manual of Correspondence (Westlake), 142–43

How to Write Letters That Win (System Company Publishers), 143

How to Write Special Feature Articles (Bleyer), 68

Humphreys, Alexander C., 29

Hustler (Vanderbilt University newspaper), 112

Huxley, Thomas Henry, 67, 135

Hyde, Grant Milnor, 116, 117. Works: *A Course in Journalistic Writing,* 68; *Handbook for Newspaper Workers,* 68, 110–11; *Newspaper Editing,* 68; *Newspaper Reporting and Correspondence,* 68

Ibsen, Henrik, 77

Idylls of the King (Tennyson), 38

"Il Penseroso" (Milton), 18

industrial journalism, 133–34

industry, demand for competent writing, 15, 26, 35, 123, 145–46

inspiration, in creative writing, 77–78

internal structure, as principle of composition, 12–13

Introduction to Rhetoric (Cairns), 67

intuition, in journalism, 105

Iowa City, writers clubs of, 91

Iowa City Press-Citizen, 118

Iowa Literary Magazine, 95

Iowa State University, 103, 133

Iowa Volunteer Infantry, 87

Iowa Writers' Workshop, 96, 97

Irving, Washington, 88. Work: *The Sketchbook,* 21

Ivanhoe (W. Scott), 19

Jackson, Andrew, 31

James, Hinton, 9

James, William, 47

Johns Hopkins University, 5

Johnson, Andrew, 40

Johnson, Burges, 73, 119

Johnson, Joseph French, 104, 115, 129, 141

Johnson, Nan, 4

Johnson, Stanley, 91

John Wilson and Sons, 113

journalism: college preparation for, 99–103; and creation of demand for writers, 14; criticism of content and style of, 30, 32–34, 106; education in reform of, 34, 106; experience of student newspapers, 112–14; influence of, 31, 32; intuition in, 105; success of, 31–32, 100

"Journalism as a Career and Educational Preparation for It" (Reid), 102

journalism courses: academic security of, 148; attention to form, 107–8, 109, 111–12, 119, 121, 147–48; attention to style, 110–11, 120, 121; enrollment of technical students in, 130; instruction in audience analysis, 108–9; instruction in editorial writing, 105–6, 107, 108, 115, 117, 118; instruction in news writing, 106, 107–8, 109–10, 111–12, 114–15, 117, 118, 119, 120; instruction in newspaper printing, 99–100; instruction in production, 115, 117–18; introduction of, 62, 63, 64, 65, 66, 67–68, 69, 70, 103–4; neglect of style, 119; practical experience in, 114–15, 117–22, 148, 151; professional writers as teachers of, 104, 116, 121; reflection of instructors'

journalism courses *(Continued)*
research interests, 111;
specialization of, 68 (*see also*
agricultural journalism;
engineering journalism;
industrial journalism);
textbooks for, 104–11;
theoretical approach in,
120–22; validity of, 105–6
"Journalism Education in the
United States," 115–16
journalism programs: course
requirements for, 66–67;
growth of, 121, 149; isolation
of, 116, 120, 121–22; liberal
arts emphasis in, 101–2,
119–20; technical and business
writing in, 124, 129–34; types
of, 115–16; vocational
emphasis in, 101, 116
The Journalism Quarterly, 120,
131–32
"Journalists, Born or Made"
(Camp), 100–101
*Journal of Business
Communication*, 146
*Journal of Technical Writing and
Communication*, ix, 146
Julius Caesar (Shakespeare),
19, 21

Kansas City Star, 91, 109
Kansas State College of
Agriculture and Applied
Science, 100
Keats, John, 38
Kendall, Amos, 31
Kenyon College, 96
Kim (Kipling), 71
King's College, 3–4. *See also*
Columbia University
Kinley, David, 127, 129
Kinne, Wisner Payne, 63, 79,
80–81
Kipling, Rudyard, 72. Work:
Kim, 71

Kirby, Richard Shelton, 27, 126
Kitzhaber, Albert R., 4, 21
Korean War, 149

The Lady of the Lake (W. Scott),
21
Lafayette College, 62, 63
Lafferty, John J., 100
Lafferty and Company Printers,
99–100
Lamb, Charles, 39
land-grant colleges: creation of, 8;
engineering programs of, 27;
journalism instruction at, 103;
purpose of, 8; segmentation of
advanced writing courses at,
63; technical writing courses
at, 130
Latin language, in classical
education, 3
law, the, and the humanities, 5,
65–66
Lawless, Greg, 113–14
Lay of the Last Minstrel (W.
Scott), 19
Lazell, Fred J., 118
Le Conte, Joseph N., 27–28
lecture and recitation method,
2–3, 4
lectures: on creative writing, 78,
80, 86, 88, 89; in journalism
courses, 115
*Lectures on Rhetoric and Belles
Lettres* (Blair), 4, 17
Lee, James Melvin, 34, 104, 115
Lee, Robert E., 99
letters, business, 142–45
The Leviathan (Hobbes), 50
LeVot, Andre, 89
Lewis, Edwin H., 66, 74, 88–89.
Work: *Business English*,
135–36
Lewis, Sinclair, 91
libel, and sensational journalism,
32
Lincoln, Abraham, 71

linguistics, in professionalized
    curriculum, 10–11, 14
Lippincott's magazine, 43
A Literary History (Wendell), 43
literature: influence of advanced
    writing courses on, 47–48; as
    model for advanced writing
    students, 43; study by
    creative writers, 66, 74, 77,
    78, 88–89, 151; study by
    students of discourse, 67;
    study by technical writers,
    135; as theme topic for
    advanced writing students,
    38, 39, 51
literature courses: growth of, 149;
    in primary and secondary
    schools, 17–18; in primary and
    secondary schools—college
    recommendations concerning,
    21–22; in professionalized
    curriculum, 10–11, 12, 13,
    14; in training of engineers,
    27, 28
little magazines, 90, 92, 95
Lloyd-Jones, Richard, 59
logic, syllogistic, 3
Logick (Hedge), 4
London, Jack, 71
Longfellow, Henry Wadsworth,
    89. Work: *Evangeline,* 21
Los Angeles Times, 109
Louisiana State University, 69,
    117–18, 126
Lounsbury, Thomas R., 26, 27.
    Work: *English Language,* 11
Lovett, Robert M., 66, 74
Lowell, James Russell, 66
Lowth, Robert. Work: *English
    Grammar,* 4
Loyola University, 153
Lyman, Rollo LaVerne, 17
Lyon, Leverett S., 127

McAnally, David Russell, 111
Macaulay, Thomas, 51, 67

Macbeth (Shakespeare), 21
McClure's magazine, 71
MacDougall, Curtis B., 120
McElroy, John G. Work: *System of
    Punctuation,* 19
McJohnston, Harrison, 141, 142
MacKaye, Percy, 93
McKee, J. H., 139
McTeague (Norris), 54
magazines: burgeoning circulation
    of, 71; and creation of
    demand for writers, 14;
    publication of fiction by,
    71–72. *See also* little
    magazines
Maher, Stuart W., III, 139
majors: system of, 8–9, 10, 11, 15;
    in writing, 152, 153–54
Making a Newspaper (Given), 105
The Making of a Journalist
    (Ralph), 104–5
Manchester, Frederick, 25
Mann, Charles Riborg, 27, 28,
    125, 134, 139
mass, as principle of composition,
    12–13, 23
Massachusetts General Court, 6
Massachusetts Institute of
    Technology (MIT), 8, 27, 28,
    134–35, 139
mass communications
    departments, 121, 149–50
Masters, Edgar Lee, 90
Matthews, Brander, 26, 88
meaning, relationship to grammar,
    25–26
Mechanics of Writing (Woolley), 67
medicine, relevance of humanities
    to, 5
memory, development of, 3, 17
Mencken, H. L., 91
Merchant of Venice (Shakespeare),
    19, 21
Meredith, George. Work: "Essay
    on Comedy," 80
Mexico, 87

Miami University (Ohio), 93
Michigan Agricultural College, 27
Middlebury College, 73, 96
Midland (journal), 95
Mill, Gordon. Work: *Technical Writing*, 145
Mill, John Stuart. Work: *Essay on Liberty*, 41
Millay, Edna St. Vincent, 74, 90. Work: "Barbara on the Beach," 74
Milton, John, 10, 18, 66, 67. Work: "Il Penseroso," 18
Mims, Edwin, 112
Minerva (newspaper), 31
Missions of the College Curriculum, 5, 124
Moise, Lionel, 91
Moore, Marianne, 90
Morgan, Edmund S., 3
Morison, Samuel Eliot, 47
Morrill Act (1862), 8, 9
Mott, Frank Luther, 14, 31, 32, 33, 71–72, 91, 95, 96, 100, 112
Mott's Times Club, 91
Mount Holyoke College, 57, 62, 63, 74
Moxley, Joseph, 97
Munson, Gorham, 90
Murphy, Lawrence W., 131–32
Murray's Grammar, 17

Naether, Carl A. Works: *A Course in English for Engineers*, 136; *The Engineer's Professional and Business Writing*, 136
narrative: instruction on, in required composition courses, 12; and journalistic writing, 107; study of, in advanced writing courses, 51, 57, 63, 67; technical, 137
Nash, Vernon, ix, 100, 119–20
Nashville, writers clubs of, 91–93

The Nation (magazine), 14, 52
National Education Association Committee of Ten, 21
National Grange, 28, 127
National Review (British journal), 40
NCTE, 103
Neal, Robert Wilson, 77–78. Work: *Short Stories in the Making*, 74–75
New Art of Writing Plays (Vega), 74
Newcomb College, 74, 89
Newman, John Henry, 135
New Orleans Item (newspaper), 118
New Orleans States (newspaper), 118
New Orleans Times-Picayune (newspaper), 118
news, definition of, 106, 107
Newspaper Editing (Hyde), 68
newspaper printing, instruction in, 99–100
Newspaper Reporting and Correspondence (Hyde), 68
newspapers: and creation of demand for writers, 14; criticism of content and style of, 30, 32–34, 106; education in reform of, 34, 106; influence of, 31, 32; partnership of journalism classes with, 117–18, 121, 151; student, 112–14, 115, 121, 151; success of, 31–32, 100; training of creative writers at, 90–91
Newspaper Writing and Editing (Bleyer), 68
news writing: exercises in, 109–10, 111; form in, 107–8, 109, 111–12, 119; practical experience in, 114–15, 117, 118, 120; standards of, 106, 107; at student newspapers,

113; style in, 111; for
technical students, 130, 131
News Writing (Spencer), 106,
107–8, 109–10
New York City, artistic community
of, 90
New York Courier and Enquirer, 33
New York *Evening Signal,* 33
New York *Evening Star,* 33
New York *Herald,* 32, 33
New York Sun, 32, 104
New York Times, 71–72, 81, 109
New York Tribune, 34, 100, 102,
132
New York University: business
writing courses at, 141, 144;
creative writing courses at,
93; journalism instruction at,
104, 133; segmentation of
advanced writing courses at,
62, 63
New York World, 14, 102, 104
Nichols, Charles Washburn, 135
Norris, Frank, 47, 54–55. Works:
McTeague, 54; *Vandover and
the Brute,* 54
North American Review, 39, 43
North Carolina State College of
Agriculture and Engineering,
131, 133
North Carolina State University,
153
Northwestern University, 127,
130, 144
Norton, Charles Eliot, 86, 102
nursing school, humanistic
training in, 65–66

O'Brien, Harry R., 128–29, 140
O'Dell, De Forest, ix, 111, 115
Of Time and the River (Wolfe),
83–85
Oklahoma Agricultural and
Mechanical College, 133
O'Neill, Eugene, 80–81. Work:
Bound East for Cardiff, 80, 90

*Origin and Development of the
Story of Troilus and Criseyde*
(Young), 68
Osgood, Charles G., 25, 56
Others magazine, 90
Our Press Gang (Wilmer), 33–34
Outcalt, Irving E., 25
Outlines of English Literature
(Shaw), 17
Outlines of Etymology (Haldeman),
11

Paintrock Road (Piper), 87
paragraph, as unit of discourse, 24
Paragraph-Writing (Scott and
Denney), 24
Paris, artistic community of, 90
Park, Clyde W. Work: *English
Applied in Technical Writing,*
138–39
Parker, Roscoe. Work: *Advanced
Exposition,* 58
Parkman, Francis, 43
Parsons, James Russell, 5
Pearsall, Thomas E. Work:
*Reporting Technical
Information,* 145
Pearson, Henry G., 58
peers, as mentors, 89–90
Pennsylvania State
College/University, 57, 95,
140, 152–53
Perkins, Max, 90
Peterson, Paul V., 121
The Philadelphia Press, 102
Philadelphia Times, 100
Philosophy of Rhetoric (G.
Campbell), 4
Piers Plowman (Middle English
poem), 103
Piper, Edwin Ford, 87–88, 95–96.
Works: *Barbed Wire,* 87;
Barbed Wire and Wayfarers,
87; *Paintrock Road,* 87
planning, study by creative
writers, 75–77

Play Making: A Manual of Craftsmanship (Archer), 77
plays. *See* drama (plays)
Poe, Edgar Allen, 74, 88, 89
Poetics (Aristotle), 80
poetry: and development of aesthetic intelligence, 72; discussion in writers' clubs, 92–93; form in, 75, 92–93, 147; peer criticism of, 89–90; planning of, 76–77; publication in little magazines, 90, 92; regional themes in, 87–88; workshops in, 78–79, 86–88, 94, 95, 96
Poetry magazine, 90
Popham, Donald F., 5–6, 18
Postal Information (Altmaier), 143
Potter, W. J., 5
Pound, Ezra, 90
Practical Journalism (Shuman), 105
The Preparation of Engineering Reports (Agg and Foster), 139
The Preparation of Reports: Engineering, Scientific, Administrative (R. P. Baker), 138, 140
primary schools: classical curriculum in, 16–17; dissatisfaction of universities with, 19–21, 35; English courses in, 17–18; incapacity of, for composition training, 34–35; reforms in English courses to suit colleges, 21–22
Princeton University, 13, 18, 56
Principles of Rhetoric (Hill), 12, 22–23, 38, 39, 40
Printer's Ink (journal), 142
printing, instruction in, 99–100
prizes, literary, 71
production, newspaper, learning of, 113–14, 115, 117–18

progressive education, and creative writing, 72–73
Provincetown Players, 87, 90
Pulitzer, Joseph, 102, 103
punctuation, entrance-level proficiency for colleges, 20
Purdue University, 28, 136
Putnam's Magazine, 39

Quincy, Josiah, 20

Radcliffe College, 79–80, 83, 85–86
Railway Age Gazette, 133
Ralegh in Guiana (Wendell), 43
Ralph, Julian. Work: *The Making of a Journalist,* 104–5
Rami Logica, 3
Ramus, Peter, 3, 4
Rankell's Remains (Wendell), 43
Ranlett, Louis F., 46
Ransom, John Crowe, 91, 92, 94
The Rat (newspaper), 112
recitation method, 2–3, 4, 17
regionalism, literary, 87–88
Reid, Whitelaw, 34, 102
Rensselaer, Steven Van, 125
Rensselaer Polytechnic Institute, 27, 125, 139
Reporting Technical Information (Houp and Pearsall), 145
"Report of the Committee on Schools of Journalism," 101–2
Report to the Corporation of Brown University, 6
Report Writing (Gaum and Graves), 138, 139
Revolutionary War, 3, 4, 17, 31
rhetoric: advanced study of, 63, 64–65, 66; in development of composition skill, 22–23; renewed interest in, 150; in training of engineers, 27
Rhetorical Grammar (J. Walker), 4

rhetoric courses: abandonment of, 1, 10–11, 15; in classical curriculum, 3; modernization of, 4

Richardson, George Francis. Works: *A Course in English for Engineers*, 136; *The Engineer's Professional and Business Writing*, 136

Rickard, T. A. Work: *A Guide to Technical Writing*, 136–37

Rideout, H. M., 11, 20

Riverside Press, 113

Robbins, Harry. Work: *Advanced Exposition*, 58

Roberts, Mary Eleanor, 78

Robespierre, 54

Robinson, Edwin Arlington, 47, 90

Robinson, Stewart, 131

Roethke, Theodore, 94

Rogers, Charles Elkins. Work: *Agricultural Journalism*, 132

Root, Charles T., 133

Ross, Earle D., 8

Rudolph, Frederick, 2, 4, 6, 7, 8, 125

Rudy, Willis, 10

Ruskin, John, 67, 135

Russell, David R., 11, 21, 36, 65, 144

Sandburg, Carl, 90, 91

Santayana, George, 47

Saturday Luncheon Club, 91

Scherer, Wilhelm, 66

School Review, 52

Schramm, Wilbur, 96

science, vocational, 125–26

scientific method, influence on classical curriculum, 3–4

Scott, Fred Newton, 25, 26, 58, 68, 148; generalized composition courses of, 63–64; on limitations of freshman composition course, 24; recognition of need for creative writing, 72; specialized composition courses of, 64–65, 66. Work: *Paragraph-Writing*, 24

Scott, Sir Walter, 38. Works: *Ivanhoe*, 19; *The Lady of the Lake*, 21; *Lay of the Last Minstrel*, 19

Scribner, Charles, 14

Scribner's (publishers), 90

Scribner's magazine, 43, 102

Scudder, Horace E., 17

secondary schools: business training in, 127; dissatisfaction of universities with, 19–21, 35; English courses in, 17–18; incapacity of, for composition training, 34–35; progressive philosophy in, 73; reforms in English courses to suit colleges, 21–22

See, Horace, 28, 134

Self, Robert T., 43, 48

sentence construction, relationship to meaning, 25–26

Serle, Ambrose, 31

Shakespeare, William, 10, 11, 13, 38, 53, 69, 77, 135. Works: *Hamlet*, 21; *Julius Caesar*, 19, 21; *Macbeth*, 21; *Merchant of Venice*, 19, 21; *Tempest*, 19

Shaw, Thomas. Work: *Outlines of English Literature*, 17

Sheffield Scientific School (at Yale), 7, 8

Shelnutt, Eve, 97

Sherman, Stuart Pratt, 142

Short Stories in the Making (Neal), 74–75

short story: form in, 74–75, 147; planning of, 75–76; workshops in, 88–89, 94

Short Story Writing (Barrett), 74

Shuman, Edwin L., 107. Work: *Practical Journalism*, 105

Silliman, Benjamin, 125
Simmons, John O., 130, 131
Sinclair, Upton, 71
The Sketchbook (Irving), 21
Smart, Walter Kay. Work: *How to Write Business Letters,* 143–44
Smith, Charles Emory, 102
Smith, Oberlin, 28, 134
Snowbound (Whittier), 21
Society for Prevention of Cruelty to Speakers (SPCS), 91
Society for the Promotion of Engineering Education, 124, 139–40
Society for Technical Communication, 146
Sowers, Leigh, 96
Spanish-American War, 87
Spencer, M. Lyle. Works: *Editorial Writing,* 105–6, 107, 108–9; *News Writing,* 106, 107–8, 109–10
Spenser, Edmund, 10, 11
The Spokane Spokesman (newspaper), 104
Springfield Republican (newspaper), 104
Sputnik educational crisis, 145, 149
Stamp Act, 31
Stanford University, 97
State Oratorical Society (Indiana), 28
Stegner, Wallace, 94, 97
Stein, Gertrude, 91
Steinmetz, Charles P., 128
Sterne, Laurence, 39
Stevens, Robert, 5
Stevens, Wallace, 90
Stevens Institute, 28, 29
Stevenson, Robert Louis. Work: *Treasure Island,* 76
Storey, Charles M., 52–53
Strauss, Abraham, 65
Strauss, Louis A., 64–65

Students' Handbook of the Facts of English Literature (Young), 68–69
style: attention of advanced writing courses to, 41–42, 46, 49–51; neglect by journalism courses, 119; rules of, as restriction on creativity, 72; rules of, in development of composition skill, 22–23, 23–25; simplicity of, in technical writing, 128; study by business writing students, 143; study by journalism students, 110–11, 120, 121; study by technical writing students, 132, 136–39
Sunday Morning Register (Eugene, Ore.), 117
Swan, C. J., 54
Swift, Jonathan, 39
Sypherd, W. O. Work: *The Engineer's Manual of English,* 138
Syracuse University, 131
System (journal), 142
System Company Publishers, 143
System of Punctuation (McElroy), 19

Taine, Hippolyte. Work: *History of English Literature,* 11
Talon, Omer, 3
Tate, Allen, 92
Teaching Creative Writing, 71, 73, 94, 97
Tebbel, John, 14–15
technical programs: degree of specialized training in, 124; growth of, 123–24, 145; literacy of students in, 124
technical writing: deficiencies in quality of, 27, 29–30; simplicity of style in, 128
Technical Writing (G. Mill), 145

technical writing courses:
academic security of, 145–46,
148; attention to form, 132,
136, 137, 138, 139, 145,
148, 151; attention to style,
132, 136–39; business
emphasis in, 135–36; demand
for, 128–29; general
education in, 134–35; growth
of, 139–40, 145, 149, 150;
instruction in audience
analysis, 138–39, 150, 151;
introduction of, 62, 63,
65–66, 68–69, 124–25;
journalistic approach in,
130–34; practical emphasis in,
148, 151; rhetorical influence
in, 150; status as specialty,
146; textbooks for, 135–39,
145; types of, 129–30
technique, study by creative
writers, 81, 82
Tempest (Shakespeare), 19
Temple University, 103
Tennyson, Alfred, Lord, 66. Work:
Idylls of the King, 38
10 Story Book (magazine), 71
Texas Agricultural and Mechanical
College, 69, 140
textbooks: for advanced writing
courses, 58; for business
writing courses, 142–44; for
creative writing courses,
74–78; for journalism
courses, 104–11; for technical
writing courses, 135–39,
145
Thackeray, William Makepeace,
13, 42
Thanet, Octave, 89
theater, experimental, 90
theme-language, 23, 37
themes: classroom criticism of, 38,
41, 45, 56, 63–64; criticism
of style in, 41–42, 49–51;
daily, 37–38, 40–41, 48–51,

54, 55; encouragement of
individuality in, 37–38
theme topics: for advanced
argumentation, 53–54; about
college life, 38–39, 51–52; for
exercises in discourse, 25;
from literature, 38, 39, 51;
and modernization of classical
curriculum, 4–5; about public
issues, 39; student-selected,
37–38, 39, 40–41, 48, 50
*The Theory and Practice of
Technical Writing* (Earle), 137
This Side of Paradise (Fitzgerald),
90
Thomas, Joseph, 63, 69
Thompson, Lawrence, 47, 93
Thurber, Edward A., 25
Thurston, Robert, 28
trade journals, 133–34
Treasure Island (Stevenson), 76
Tufts University, 139
Tulane College, 74, 112
Turnbull, Andrew, 89–90
Turneaure, F. E., 29
*Twenty Years of School and College
English*, 18–19
Tyndall, John, 135
Types of News Writing (Bleyer),
68, 106, 107

Union College, 56–57
unity, as principle of composition,
12–13, 23, 24
universities. *See* higher education;
land grant colleges; under
name of specific college or
university
University Daily Kansan, 115
The University Missourian
(newspaper), 115
University of California, Berkeley,
27–28
University of Chicago: advanced
writing courses at, 55–56, 74;
business program at, 127;

University of Chicago *(Continued)*
creative writing courses at,
73–74, 88–89; journalism
instruction at, 103;
progressive philosophy at, 73;
segmentation of advanced
writing courses at, 66–67;
student newspaper at, 112
University of Cincinnati, 139
University of Delaware, 126
University of Florida, 69, 126,
133, 149
University of Georgia, 126
University of Illinois: business
program at, 127; business
writing courses at, x, 129,
140–41, 142, 144; creative
writing courses at, 73–74;
specialized composition
courses at, 69; technical
writing courses at, 133
University of Indiana, 103
University of Iowa: creative
writing courses at, ix–x, 69,
73–74, 86–88, 89, 95–96;
journalism instruction at,
103, 118; literary magazines
at, 95
University of Kansas: advanced
writing courses at, 57;
journalism instruction at,
103, 111, 114–15;
specialized composition
courses at, 69; technical
writing courses at, 139
University of Maine, 149
University of Maryland, 149
University of Michigan, 29, 148;
creative writing courses at,
73, 74, 93; generalized
advanced writing courses at,
63–64; journalism instruction
at, 103; professionalization of
curriculum of, 7;
segmentation of advanced
writing courses at, 63, 64–66

University of Minnesota, 63, 69,
126, 130, 135, 140
University of Missouri: creative
writing courses at, 73, 95;
journalism instruction at, ix,
100, 103, 104, 111, 115;
technical programs at, 126
University of Montana, 130
University of Nebraska, 73, 87,
103, 144
University of North Carolina,
9–10, 11
University of North Dakota, 103
University of Oregon, 103, 117
University of Pennsylvania:
advanced writing courses at,
55; business program at, 127;
entrance exams at, 19; impact
of professionalization on
English courses, 11;
journalism instruction at,
103, 104, 115; specialized
composition courses at, 69
University of Southern California,
144
University of Tennessee, 126, 149,
153
University of Wisconsin: business
program at, 127; business
writing courses at, 141, 144;
creative writing courses at,
95; journalism instruction at,
103; segmentation of
advanced writing courses at,
67–69; technical writing
courses at, 133, 135
University of Wyoming, 149

Van Buren, Martin, 31
Vanderbilt University, 94, 112
Vandover and the Brute (Norris),
54
Vega, Lope de. Work: *New Art of
Writing Plays,* 74
Velocipedist (magazine), 14
Verse Writing (Carruth), 72, 75

vers libre, 92
Veysey, Laurence, 8–9, 124, 125
The Vicar of Wakefield
 (Goldsmith), 19
Virgil, 6
The Vision of Sir Launfal, 21

Walker, Franklin, 54–55
Walker, John. Work: *Rhetorical
 Grammar*, 4
Wallace, Una, 87–88
Washington College, 99–100
Washington Square Book Shop, 90
Washington Square Players, 90
Watergate scandal, 149
Watt, Homer. Work: *The
 Composition of Technical
 Papers*, 137–38
Wayland, Francis, 6
Wayside Monthly, 71
Webb, James Watson, 33
Webster, Daniel, 112
Webster, Edward Harlan, 127
Webster, Noah, 31
Weeks, Francis W., x, 141, 142
Wellesley College, 94
Wells, H. G., 44
Wendell, Barrett, 58, 66, 74, 79,
 89, 90; composition courses
 of, 12–13, 23, 37, 40–43,
 47–52, 55, 57, 60, 63, 70,
 86; on limitations of freshman
 composition course, 23–24;
 professional background of,
 42–43; recognition of need
 for creative writing, 72.
 Works: *The Duchess Emilia*,
 42, 43; *English Composition*,
 12, 23, 55; *A Literary
 History*, 43; *Ralegh in
 Guiana*, 43; *Rankell's
 Remains*, 43
Wesleyan College, 73, 96
Westlake, J. Willis. Work: *How to
 Write Letters: A Manual of
 Correspondence*, 142–43

West Point military academy, 125
Wharton, Edith, 89
Wharton School of Business, 104,
 115, 127
Whately, Richard. Work: *Elements
 of Rhetoric*, 4
The Wheelman (magazine), 14
The Wheelman's Gazette, 14
Wheelwright, Edwin March, 52–53
White, Andrew D., 2, 102
White, Emerson, 28
White, Horace, 100
White, J. G., 128
Whitman, Walt, 135
Whittier, John Greenleaf, 43, 89.
 Work: *Snowbound*, 21
Wilbers, Stephen, x, 87, 88, 96
Wilbur, Richard, 94
Wiley, H. W., 29–30
Wilkins, Mary E., 89
Wilkinson, William, 66
Will, Allen Sinclair, 116
Williams, Sara L., x, 115
Williams, Talcot, 104
Williams, Walter, 104
Williams College, 57
Wilmer, Lambert, 33–34. Work:
 Our Press Gang, 33–34
Wilson, Albert Frederick, 133
Wilson, Edmund, 89, 90
Wilson, Logan, 5
Wingate, Charles F., 100
Winnick, R. H., 47, 93
Winterowd, Ross, 152
Witt, Peter D., 18
Witte, Stephen P., 98
Wolfe, Thomas, 83–85, 93. Work:
 Of Time and the Rover, 83–85
women's colleges, creative writing
 courses at, 74
Woodward, Bob, 149
Woolley, Edwin, 116. Works:
 Exercises in English, 67;
 Handbook of Composition, 67,
 110–11; *Mechanics of Writing*,
 67; *Written English*, 67

World War II, 145, 149, 151
Wozniak, John Michael, 10, 13, 18, 55, 63
writers: as mentors for other writers, 89–90; professional, as teachers of creative writing, 93–94, 96–97, 98, 149; professional, as teachers of journalism, 104, 116, 121
writers' clubs, 91–93
writing: demand created by industrial revolution for, 15; establishment as profession, 14–15, 71–72
writing-across-the-curriculum movement, 150, 152, 153
Writing for the Trade Press (Farrington), 133–34
Writing the Short-Story (Esenwein), 75–76
Written English (Woolley), 67

Yale College: classical curriculum at, 2; creative writing courses at, 86; enrollment figures, 5; entrance exams at, 18; humanities in technical training at, 27; professionalization of curriculum of, 7, 8; revision of classical curriculum at, 4; technical programs at, 125, 126
Yeats, William Butler, 71
yellow journalism, 32–34
Young, Karl, 68–69, 135. Works: *Century Readings for a Course in English Literature*, 68; *Essays for College Men: Education, Science, and Art*, 68; *Freshman English: A Manual*, 68; *Origin and Development of the Story of Troilus and Criseyde*, 68; *Students' Handbook of the Facts of English Literature*, 68–69
The Youth's Companion (magazine), 46

Steven Aupied

About the Author

Katherine H. Adams is an associate professor of English and assistant academic vice president at Loyola University in New Orleans. She was director of the writing-across-the-curriculum program there for five years. She has co-written an advanced composition textbook, *The Accomplished Writer*, and co-edited an anthology of essays, *Teaching Advanced Composition: Why and How*, with John L. Adams. Her articles on teaching writing have appeared in *College Composition and Communication*, *Rhetoric Review*, *Rhetoric Society Quarterly*, *The Writing Instructor*, and other journals. She is currently co-authoring a grammar handbook for Houghton Mifflin with Michael L. Keene.

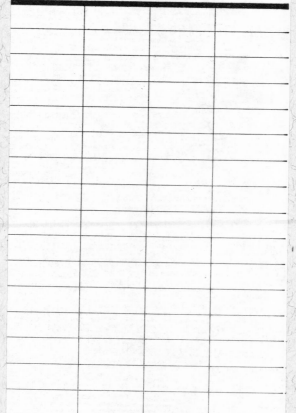

DATE DUE
